The
Universe
Within Us

The
Universe
Within Us

A Guide to the Purpose of Life

by

JANE E. HARPER

Bahá'í
PUBLISHING

Wilmette, Illinois

Bahá'í Publishing
401 Greenleaf Avenue, Wilmette, Illinois 60091-2844

Copyright © 2009 by the National Spiritual Assembly
of the Bahá'ís of the United States

17   16   15   14   5   4   3   2

Library of Congress Cataloging-in-Publication Data

Harper, Jane E.
  The universe within us : a guide to the purpose of life / by Jane E. Harper.
      p. cm.
  Includes bibliographical references and index.
  ISBN 978-1-931847-58-2
  1. Bahai Faith. 2. Spirituality—Bahai Faith. 3. Life cycle, Human—Religious
aspects—Bahai Faith. 4. Spirituality. 5. Life cycle, Human—Religious aspects. I.
Title.

BP370.H365 2009
297.9'3—dc22

                                        2009000921

For Dad

Acknowledgments

To Sherry Lester, for her ability to appreciate this work even in its embryonic stage, her insistence that I finish, and for reading more renditions of this book than is reasonable to expect. (If I am the mother of this book, she is certainly its grandmother.) To my sister, Anne Harper, for her genuine intrigue with the book's myriad topics, and for understanding what I was talking about, even when I was rambling on about newly forming ideas. (She is certainly this book's Aunt Anne.) To Phyllis Ring, for her sharp mind, her enthusiastic encouragement, and her excellent grammar. To Julie Weiss, for her timely formation of the Women's Writers Group, her patience when this project disappeared from view, and her invaluable and speedy feedback on manuscript revisions in the eleventh hour. To Sonia Connor and Susan Duffy, who listened to their share of the manuscript, much of which fell under my own editor's knife. To Ronnie Tomanio, who—although he claims not to remember this—commented about the previous manuscript, "Who is this written for, people from Alpha Centauri?" (Now, Ronnie, it is written for earthlings.) To the hardworking team at the Bahá'í Publishing Trust—Terry Cassiday, Christopher Martin, and Ariana Brown—who helped make this dream a reality. To Paul Roberts and Julie Pardus-Oakes for their gracious flexibility with my work schedule during the revision phase. And finally, my most loving appreciation goes to my husband, Mark Tucker, for his steady support, his faith in my abilities, and for building with me a joyful home, which allowed me to find my focus and finally complete this book.

I would also like to extend my gratitude to all those scientists and scholars who write books about their own field of expertise for the interested layperson and who have translated the world's ancient and sacred texts into English. These people have put worlds of knowledge and ideas within my reach. Without them, this book would not have been possible.

Contents

Introduction

"It's about the size of a pencil eraser," my father said calmly, as my stomach dropped away in shock and fear.

He was describing the tumor that had been found on his spine.

This was not his first encounter with cancer. Five years earlier it had finally been discovered, after months of undiagnosed pain, that he had prostate cancer, and his death sentence had been pronounced at that time. I dealt with the enormity of the situation by going into a type of denial. This was, after all, a man who had hardly ever been sick in his life, and never with anything serious. Denial, holding my breath, and hoping for the best was a combination that seemed to serve me well at the time. In fact, his cancer soon went into remission, and life returned to normal. Five years later, enough time had passed for me to believe that the doctors had made some kind of mistake. Until now.

During those five years, however, much had changed for me. I had been investigating the teachings of Bahá'u'lláh, the Prophet-Founder of the Bahá'í Faith, and my contemplation of these teachings had led me again and again to the realization of their truth.

Five years before, I had gone into denial. What else did I have but faith in the ultimate physical fitness of my father? Or in the medical establishment's ability to vanquish that which threatened his life?

But now I had the rudimentary beginnings of a faith of another sort—one based on study and comprehension. It was a faith that helped me understand how this material world and our transient physical lives fit into a much larger scenario, a spiritual reality that surrounds, includes, and informs all things. This time, I could lean on my new faith for support, for succor, and for information.

As my father's cancer proceeded to ravage his body and it became apparent that this time there would be no cure except by miracle, I felt in my inmost heart

1

the need to offer him some kind of solace, to share with him some of what I had been learning.

Neither of us ever spoke of the fact that he was dying. He was not in denial about it himself. In fact, in typical take-charge fashion, he had gone to the funeral parlor one day and selected his own coffin.

But between the two of us, the words were never spoken. The comfort I needed to offer had to be in a form that would not break our unspoken pact. And so I wrote what I considered a logical treatise proving that there is a part of every human being that survives death. I sent it to him and asked him to read it, explaining that I was considering selling it for publication. It was a thin ruse, I know, but he allowed it.

I don't remember that he ever talked to me about the subject of the essay. His only response was that it sounded "like that 'Abdu'l-Bahá guy," a reference to the son and appointed successor of Bahá'u'lláh, Whose writings I had recently introduced to my father.

As it turned out, that essay made its biggest impact on me. It sounded logical, but I had written it quickly. Could it actually be proven? Was I just kidding myself, or could I back it up with research? Would contemporary science contradict or confirm my assumptions? Would Bahá'u'lláh's teachings—which had made so much about this clear to me—and scientific findings contradict or confirm each other?

Bahá'u'lláh states that there is no contradiction between science and religion. I instinctively recognized the truth of this. Religion and science are both systems of inquiry that lead to truth. And how can truth contradict truth? When pursued correctly, both must inevitably lead to the same conclusion. Philosophically this made sense, but I had not yet proved it for myself.

Bahá'u'lláh exhorts us to investigate reality for ourselves. This would require me not to believe blindly in that which the thinkers and leaders of the day proclaim to be true, be they scientist, priest, or politician. While I could certainly consider their opinions, I ultimately needed to figure out what I believed for myself.

Beyond that, clear understanding of what is, exactly, a human being, is critically important in its own right. For what better determines our behavior than our belief about what a human being is or the purpose for our existence? Clearly, if we are sophisticated animals without a spiritual nature, what is the point of living a virtuous and moral life? But if we are spiritual in nature, then this life is just one phase of existence and not our final destination. If this life is only the first phase, then there could be a very good reason for living a virtuous life.

The process of my father's dying was emotionally consuming, exhausting, and intense. I watched this once vital and strong man, the very epitome of masculine virility, have his physical powers seep away little by little.

It was obvious that he was totally unprepared for facing his death. Nothing in his personal repertoire could ease his emotional pain. He shored himself up by sheer strength of will, but it was a brittle facade.

As his health declined, the day came when he could no longer leave his bed. One day he required a blood transfusion, and an ambulance was called to bring him to the hospital for his appointment. Two strong ambulance attendants moved my father from his bed to the stretcher and into the ambulance. It was a huge blow, watching this independent man so reduced in capacity and now so dependent on others—strangers, even.

At the hospital, his blood pressure was so low that the nurse giving him the transfusion had a hard time finding a vein in which to insert the needle. After some tense moments, the transfusion began. There lay my father, trying to keep in good humor but looking very tired, drawn, and frail.

I wanted so badly to offer him some kind of comfort, but how was I to comfort my own father? I had never in my life been called on to perform such a task. But now there seemed such a great need. I blundered forward and, calling upon my newfound beliefs, suggested he call upon his own parents, who had passed on many years prior, for assistance.

Tears sprang to his eyes. He squeezed them shut and grimaced. I watched in dismay as he purposefully clamped down and subdued every emotion that threatened to breach that wall of will. Moments later, blinking away the vanguard tears, he opened his eyes. His emotions subdued and vanquished, he was once again master of his feelings.

At that moment, I felt embarrassed that I would say the exact thing that would give him pain when my intent was to say that which would give him comfort. Yet, over the years, as I recalled that scene, I have often wondered where his response came from.

Was it that I had asked a once self-reliant and strong man to admit helplessness? Was his weakness too much of a corrosion of his self-identity, an identity that revolved around the ideals of masculine strength? As his physical strength had ebbed away, had it taken with it that which my father considered "self"?

Or was I simply asking him to reach for something he could not be sure was there?

As I watched his struggle, I couldn't help but wonder whether it had to be like this. It was as if he had been tossed into the ocean and suddenly needed to learn how to swim. After all, if there is one unshakable truth that we cannot deny, it is that everybody dies. And yet our only preparation for it is to never think about it. Millions of people enter this time with less preparation and less study than is made for qualifying for a driver's license.

Isn't there anything to be learned while our personal waters are calm that would assist us when things swirl out of control? I'm talking about the kind of learning that satisfies both the heart and the intellect. So much of what many religions teach cannot withstand intellectual scrutiny. And so much of what science teaches cannot explain why a material creature such as myself has so many abstract, non-material dimensions.

I believe my father, both religion and science having failed him, had composed his own view of life and its purpose. He shared very few of his inmost beliefs with me, except such biological factoids as "You are the end result of a long line of survivors, who lived long enough to pass on their DNA," which indicated Darwinian leanings. These leanings did not help him in his moment of need, and I am convinced that if he had found a way to truly understand that he was spiritual in nature, and not just a material being, it might have transformed his experience, eased his fears, and given him something to depend on besides his own willpower and courage.

The experience of my father's final months convinced me that now was the time to investigate the question of what exactly a human being is, while I was young and well, and to not let it wait until I was too preoccupied with my own dying to give it the study it needs and deserves.

I began to read books on everything from physics to human behavior. I studied the Bahá'í writings. Many of my beliefs were refined, others discarded, and new ones formed. My essay, I felt, needed to become a book. I knew I was onto something. What this thing was, I wasn't sure, yet it dogged me and refused to leave me alone. I took notes. I wrote. I drew pictures of circles within circles. I walked. I thought. I meditated. I prayed.

One night I dreamed that 'Abdu'l-Bahá was laughing and laughing—great big roaring belly laughs. I knew that he was laughing about "the book." Although I didn't know whether or not he was laughing at my book, my feeling, upon awakening, was that I needed to write a book so good, so accurate, that 'Abdu'l-Bahá would not laugh *at* it, but would laugh because it had made him happy.

The length of this book in no way conveys the complexity of the subject at hand. My intent is to give, as briefly as possible, a comprehensive overview of life and its purpose. This has been a bigger challenge to me than to let it swell to a thousand pages—something it could easily do. More has been cut from this book and lies in discarded notes, scraps of paper, paragraphs, and chapters than what remains. And what remains, I hope, is that overview, expressed as succinctly and as directly as possible.

The title of this book is drawn from the following quote attributed to the Imam Alí*:

Dost thou reckon thyself only a puny form
When within thee the universe is folded?[1]

I experienced one of those "eureka" moments upon hearing these words, and in an instant, my understanding of what defines a human being was changed.

But what does this quotation mean exactly, and how can a human being enfold the universe? Let me assure you, the Imam Alí spoke a literal truth. How exactly you enfold the universe and what that implies about your long-term future are explored in the following pages.

---

* The first imam, the Prophet Muḥammad's appointed successor.

1

The Universe

"There's the Big Dipper," says my dad.

He is looking up, his arm outstretched, pointing into the night sky. We are standing by the garage door, having just arrived home from a family outing of ice cream cones while watching planes land at the local airport. My mom has taken my little brother inside to put him to bed. But I'm six years old now, old enough to stay outside and look at the stars with my dad. I follow his gaze, look out past his fingertip, up to the stars scattered across the heavens.

I didn't know it then, but when I followed his gaze toward the Big Dipper, I was gazing out to infinity.

Some people naturally look up. They are the wonderers. My dad was a wonderer. And when he pointed upward, out into infinity, it felt like a natural direction for me, the way my head was supposed to tilt.

Years later, my friends and I would try to imagine "forever." Forever and ever and ever. We were trying to imagine infinity, and it made my head feel very odd and ticklish. I had to shake it, shake out my whole body and laugh. Get back to normal. Get back to now.

I was also a big rock collector in my childhood. (So, yes, I could look down as well.) I couldn't keep away from picture books that described continent formation or volcanic eruptions and earthquakes. I was fascinated with paleontology—the study of prehistoric life and environments. I lived in a valley that had once been a glacial lake, a fact that sparked my imagination. Before that, the valley had been covered by an immense ice sheet. Before that, unfamiliar animals had roamed. Before that, mountains stood higher than the Himalayas. Before that, there was only barren rock, devoid of life. Before that, everything was hot and crackly. Before that . . .

Somehow, looking backwards was easier than looking forwards. At least when I was going backwards, I had something to look at. But I knew that infinity worked in both directions.

These were only two aspects of my attempts to map the universe I had found myself in and turn it into something I could understand. We all do this to some degree. We try to map out the world and create models that tell a person, "You are here." A good model tells us where we came from, where we are headed, and—most importantly—what the whole point is, anyway.

But infinity is a big place. There's lots of room for variety. Models and maps inevitably differ from one culture to another, and every person's model will be unique, at least in its details. In truth, it's not actually possible to contain infinity in a model any more than it's possible to contain a country in a map. Our maps and models are only representative, something people put together to help them navigate. We use them to understand where we are, how to get to an intended destination, and maybe what to expect when we get there. But we shouldn't expect England to be the color orange because it's that color on the map, and we will be hard-pressed to actually locate those black boundary lines that delineate a nation's boundaries. However we map out the universe, we shouldn't confuse our models with the real thing.

The drive behind all this mapmaking and model-building, though, should be the hunger to know the difference between what is imagined to be real and what is actually real. Not the hunger to be sure (some of the most closed-minded people I know are blessed with assurance), but the hunger to constantly push back that reef of ignorance that separates us from the ocean of knowledge. In this condition, it doesn't matter what culture a person is born in or how a person is raised. Wonder, openness, and opportunity can lead anyone ever closer to the truth. And in this condition, the map changes as the mapmaker changes.

But it has to start somewhere.

In the Beginning

I was born into a Catholic family, baptized when I was only a few weeks old, and dutifully raised and educated as a Catholic. The Catholic Church has its own way of describing the world, and I officially began to learn this description in the first grade.

According to the nuns who taught me, God had brought the universe into being in six days, during which He created the first man and woman—Adam and Eve. They lived in paradise, where all their needs were met and suffering was unknown. Only one act was forbidden them—to eat the fruit from the tree of knowledge.

The promise, however, that eating the fruit would make them like gods was too compelling for the couple, and they ate. God eventually found them out and angrily drove Adam and Eve from paradise, out into the world where they had to fend for themselves, suffer, and know death. Eve, along with all her female descendants, was saddled with the special curse of suffering pain during childbirth.

I was also told that we are all stained by that first sin of our first ancestors and that we are, as a result, all born in a condition of "original sin." This original sin can be removed, however, through the sacrament of baptism, a ritual in which water is poured over a person's head while a priest says special prayers. All babies born in the Catholic Church are baptized within weeks of birth, lest they die and go to limbo, a type of holding tank for unbaptized innocents, which my childish mind visualized as a vast, airy ocean teeming with babies.

After baptism, life in the Catholic world becomes ever more complex, filled with rituals and sacraments designed to ward off the ever-looming threat of hell, a place of eternal torment to which my soul would be consigned after death if I failed to live the prescribed Catholic life.

I also learned that, as a female child, I was born doubly tainted, for not only was I born in sin, but my femaleness itself was a deficiency. This was never fully explained to me, but I always noticed that the priests, monsignors, and bishops—all of whom were male—were the ones who strode about confidently and issued the orders. When the bishop came to visit our church, it was a big deal. When the monsignor came to our class to hand out report cards, it was a very serious affair. The monsignor would pick up each card, call out each name, and review the grades as each student made his or her way, confidently or timidly, to the front of the class. As he handed the card to each student with a slight frown, a weak smile, or a comment to try harder, it felt as if God Himself were judging us.

The nuns who taught me were solemn enough and demanded absolute obedience, but the clergy clearly had a higher level of authority. The clergy—who were all men—ruled. They made decisions and issued orders, while the women were expected to submit and cater to them.

In fact, the ideal female as described by the Church was a caricature of saintliness. At least, that was how I visualized her. She was expected to be quietly supportive of men, humble, devout, faithful, innocent, trusting, modest, chaste, and eternally patient. I pictured her then as I picture her now: kneeling, hands clasped in prayer, eyes raised to the heavens. When she is not praying, she is feeding the poor, wiping the sweat from the brow of her hardworking husband, and tending the sick. I thought I would need to become this impossible idealized woman in order to be accepted and loved by God and by others.

I learned that if I were perfectly good and without sin, after I died I would be rewarded by being welcomed into heaven—a good place up in the sky, above the clouds somewhere, where the weather was always pleasant. The souls in heaven are near God, and angels are always singing. Everyone in heaven would be singing, lounging about, and being happy.

I also learned that if I were bad, I would be sent to hell after I died. Hell was located deep within the bowels of the earth. It was very hot there, its main topography consisting of flames and rivers of poison. The souls in hell were ruled and tormented by Satan—he who tempts the unwary from the true life prescribed by the Church. The soul who was sent to hell would suffer eternal torment, for there was no release from this punishment—ever.

I assumed I would end up in the third location for departed souls—a place called purgatory. I never could conjure up a location for purgatory. All I understood was that it was a temporary, pay-for-your-sins place between hell and heaven for us small-time sinners.

Quite early on, I knew very well that I wasn't good enough for heaven. After all, I fought regularly with my sisters and brother, and I was not above lying to get out of trouble. I figured the best I could do as a Catholic—where heaven was pretty much barred to all except an elite few—would be to try to stay out of hell and minimize my time in purgatory.

He Who Dies with the Most Stuff Wins

What I gathered from my culture about my life and its purpose helped round out my worldview. Born in the mid-fifties in a small New England town, I learned I was living in a very competitive world. People put most of their time, thought, and activity into being prettier, faster, smarter, or wealthier than their neighbors. Siblings competed for parental attention and approval, students competed with each other for the best grades, athletes competed with each other to win contests, workers competed against each other to earn promotions, and the list went on.

The more competitive one was, and the more one was willing to work harder than everyone else, the greater one's success would be. Those who didn't succeed simply didn't try hard enough. The rich had earned their riches, and the poor were lazy. Since there could only be a few top positions (if we were all on top there'd be no "top"), the climb through the ranks required a hard, consuming, and relentless struggle.

Furthermore, I learned that, as a female, I was less capable physically and intellectually, less rational, and more emotional than my male counterparts. In other words, I was weak, irrational, and guided by my feelings. Fortunately for me, men supposedly liked these feminine quirks, or were at least willing to put up with them if they were presented in a pretty enough package. The female purpose, I learned, was to marry and raise a family. Happiness and fulfillment would be found in these pursuits. It would also add to my happiness to live in a nice house with a large yard, to have at least one car, a television, and all the latest conveniences. In other words, having lots of stuff was deemed essential for happiness.

As a woman-to-be, I saw that the things I ought most to crave were jewelry and fine clothes. Beauty and popularity would also make me happy, as would parties and other large social gatherings. The biggest event of my life would be my wedding day, in which all that was precious to my female heart would gloriously come together.

My culture didn't really offer an opinion about what would happen to me after death. What I did absorb was that it didn't matter what happened then as long as I had lived a full life. If I had done all the right things, as outlined above, I would be able to look back on my life with satisfaction. And that, I was assured, would be enough.

An Accident Waiting to Happen

Of course, there is more to education than religion and culture. As I began to study the sciences, I found a very different view of the universe, life, and its purpose.

The sciences viewed the universe not as the creation of an all-powerful God but as an *accident*, the result of an initial explosion called the Big Bang. It even viewed *me* as an accident and just another animal among many. Its evolutionary theories taught me that all life, including human life, was the result of a series of random events, beginning with lightning striking the primordial ooze at just the right moment.

According to the scientific view, no guiding intelligence had brought me into existence. Indeed, the fact that life existed at all was highly improbable, for every tenuous step life took to insinuate itself on this planet was constantly under assault and could have been wiped out at any moment by that same capricious hand of chance that had brought it into existence in the first place.

Death was the end of the road for me—at least "me" as I think of myself—according to science. Since science defined me as a biological composition of atoms and molecules performing a myriad of juxtaposed biochemical processes, this "me"—those atoms and molecules—would find their way into other compositions after my death. My atoms and molecules, recycled from time immemorial, would be recycled yet again in a different form after I breathed my last.

I also learned that I was a competitive animal and that human beings obey an essential law of evolution—survival of the fittest. My existence had no purpose at all—except, perhaps, to eat or be eaten and to live long enough to pass on my DNA. In this view of the world, neighbor vies with neighbor, and nation vies against nation. As I grew up during the Cold War and came of age at the end of the Vietnam War, I found that examples of our animal-like behavior were in no short supply.

When Worlds Collide

These were the models—the Catholic, cultural, and scientific—with which I was instilled. They didn't always mesh neatly, and sometimes they even rubbed uncomfortably against each other. For example, even though the Catholic and cultural models had some common features (such as the inferiority of women to men), as did the scientific and cultural models (which both say that human beings are competitive by nature), the scientific and Catholic models stood at marked odds with each other. The scientific model, for instance, did not mention the existence of a Creator, whereas the Catholic model had God, the Creator, at the center of everything.

In the sixth grade, when I began learning the scientific theories of the earth's formation and evolution of species, this collision made me terribly uncomfortable. I wanted these two descriptions to fit together neatly, but they simply didn't. Fortunately for me, a lay substitute teacher, Mrs. Donovan, taught us this subject. She didn't scare me like the nuns did, so I asked her about the difference between the biblical six days and what science taught.

It was a question I'd never have dared ask the nuns. They were rigid and stern and had long ago frightened me into silence. I knew very well that those things that couldn't be explained rationally had to be accepted on faith, that questioning the Church teachings was a sure path to hell, and that my question had "doubt" written all over it.

Mrs. Donovan explained, rather neatly I think, that each day in the Bible represented millions of years. I could live with this explanation, although why the Bible didn't just say "in the first hundred million years" opened up a whole other avenue of questions.

Despite my fears about going to hell for questioning what I was being taught, I couldn't stop thinking. Silently I asked myself many questions. How could baptism—basically splashing water on a person's head—make any difference whether that person went to heaven or hell? Where did the sacraments come from? Who came up with the idea of original sin? Where did all the prayers come from? If God was all-knowing, why didn't He know Adam and Eve would eat the fruit, or why wasn't He at least aware of when they were actually eating it?

Then one day around the age of thirteen, while I was sitting quietly at mass, a rebellious thought passed through my mind: "If God wanted me to believe everything the priests and nuns say, wouldn't He have given them a brain and me a tape recorder?" Since God *had* given me a brain, I concluded, that must mean He wanted me to use it. It was a shocking thought, which came to me before I knew what was happening. And it stuck.

Outwardly I remained silent and obedient, but inwardly revolt stirred. My questions and observations punched hole after hole in the Church's explanation of the universe and life's purpose. By the time I had reached adulthood, the Catholic paradigm resembled a colander, with so many holes that it could barely hold anything, least of all my attention.

The cultural model I had grown up with took longer for me to discard. Although as a girl, I believed I would grow up, get married at a young age, and have children (I considered a twenty-one-year-old unmarried neighbor an old maid), I wasn't exactly looking forward to it. I loved climbing trees, playing adventure games in the woods, or turning my bicycle into a horse with a piece of clothesline tied to the handlebars. I couldn't imagine that someday I would want to swap my jeans for a skirt, sneakers for heels, and become preoccupied with my hair. It seemed to me it would take some kind of magic spell for me to want to make such a swap, and I looked to my future with dread instead of longing.

I was well into my twenties before I finally understood that what was promoted by my culture and what actually results in happiness are two different things. People can get married and not find happiness. People can have children and not find happiness. People can acquire lots of material things and not be happy. If a woman's happiness is to be found in marriage and child-rearing, why, I wondered, were so many women seeking fulfillment outside the home? If working hard to acquire goods and status was so fulfilling, why were people so tired and irritable instead of vital and happy? Why did so few people flourish under such a system? Why was there so much poverty? Why was there so much alcoholism? Why was there so much crime?

THE UNIVERSE WITHIN US

Internal development, it seemed to me, was being sacrificed for the acquisition of material goods and social standing. After all, how could we claim to be living up to our fullest potential if our emotional, psychological, intellectual, and spiritual dimensions were not actively engaged and utilized? I could only conclude that those things valued and promoted by Western culture do not necessarily produce happiness. In fact, I realized that these things veer us way off course and away from that which promotes a true understanding of ourselves and our purpose and which ultimately leads to true happiness.

It takes only a few questions to reveal some serious flaws in both the Catholic and cultural models. In fact, most people I know have no problem with discarding parts of the models that they disagree with and developing an individual model that works for them. Nevertheless, the risk here is that one might discard the parts that actually represent reality and keep the parts that are based on fantasy. Likewise, the models we each construct may have more bearing on personal preference than reality. In the end, the individual models we construct may no more reflect reality than what we have discarded as false.

Knowledge Is a Work in Progress

Certain doubts often arise about the scientific model, as well. If our nature is totally animalistic, if we are designed to gain the advantage over our fellows, even at the cost of their lives, then why don't warfare and conflict create health and happiness?

Only a fool can deny that war is a cause of human misery and debasement. Gaining advantage, being victorious over the opponent, is often the source of regret and great emotional suffering. I've listened to many veterans of war tell their stories and have lost count of the number who cry, even fifty years later, at their recollections.

The scientific model looks at the human being as an animal trying to carve out its niche and survive in a hostile world. But the sciences hardly have the last word on anything, and once I started to understand this, I began to view the scientific description of life and its purpose with a wary eye. Over the years, I have watched as one scientific theory replaced another. Yesterday's certainty is today's nonsense, and sometimes it's the other way around, as yesterday's nonsense becomes today's certainty.

I have been interested in the sciences since I was very young. A wonderful book called *The World We Live In, Volume 1: The First Four Billion Years* sparked my imagination. It was one of those beautifully illustrated "Life" books published by Time (they currently call them TIME-LIFE books). This particular book has a publication date of 1962. I know this because I still have the book and still enjoy studying its illustrations. I was six years old at the time of its printing.

The colorful and vivid paintings in its pages detail the earliest days of Earth. Over the years, I am sure I have spent hours looking at those illustrations, inserting myself into them, imagining myself there. Thanks to the artists (and the older I become, the more my gratitude to them grows), I've been present at the earth's formation, its cooling, the first rains, the development of the continents and oceans, and the development and evolution of life. I have watched life develop in the oceans and creep onto the land. I have even been horrified by the grotesque sight of an Allosaurus consuming its bloody prey (although this was on a fold-out page, so I didn't have to be horrified unless I wanted to be).

One particular illustration gives me a special kind of Godlike view, for it shows a spiral of earths and depicts the entire course of our planet's life, from beginning to end. In this scene, the earth emerges red-hot from a cloud of glowing gases and slowly cools, turning from red to brown, and then to the familiar green, blue, and white of the modern Earth. The continents become recognizable as soon as the oceans and continents form, and they remain the same throughout the earth's lifespan, with only a few variations as time passes. At various points, major ice ages are depicted, and the Northern Hemisphere is dominated by white. At other points, the northern ice cap is small, and the oceans have invaded the continents, shrinking land masses and flooding portions of their interiors. The ice ages come and go, the oceans shrink and expand, until the earth fades away, smaller and smaller, back to glowing red, representing the time of our sun's death. Finally the Earth fades away to the dark and lifeless orb it will become four billion years in the future.

By 1975, when I was a freshman in college, the certainty that the continents had formed in the early epoch of planet formation was being threatened with a new hypothesis. My college geology textbook, printed in 1969, presents a less stable picture of the earth, one in which the continents are moving across the face of the planet at a rate of one or two centimeters each year. At some point in the distant past, the Americas and Eurasia / Africa were much closer together than they are today. In fact, the textbook showed that there had once been a time when the continents were a single land mass that split and gradually moved apart. The pros and cons of this theory, called continental drift, are discussed in detail in this textbook, with the author weighing in on the continental drift side.

I recently borrowed another Time book called *The Third Planet*, which has a publication date of 1989, from my local library. No pros and cons are discussed here, and pages and pages are devoted to the mechanisms of continental drift.

The current theory—now called plate tectonics—describes a process in which the continents have collided and split apart multiple times over the past two billion years. Oceans, mountain ranges, faults, earthquakes, and volcanoes are all attributed to the moving plates upon which the continents rest. As these plates ram into each other, mountain ranges are formed. Earthquake-prone regions sit where plates collide and the edge of one is forced beneath the other.

The Atlantic Ocean formed as the plates moved away from each other. The mid-Atlantic ridge, a mountain range that runs down the center of the ocean, pushes the Americas and Eurasia / Africa apart as new material from deep inside the earth pushes its way up and out onto the seafloor. It has taken eons for the continents and oceans to achieve the configurations we are familiar with today, a configuration that turns out to be only temporary in geologic terms. This planet, it turns out, is very, very busy.

Somehow, between 1962 and 1989, our conceptions about the stability of the continents changed dramatically. We went from no mention of traveling continents, to the consideration of the pros and cons of the theory, to elaborate descriptions of how continents move.

"Continental displacement"—the idea that the continents once belonged to a single land mass that was forced apart—was formally proposed in 1912 by German scientist Alfred Wegener. He supported his theory by pointing out the similarities between rocks, plants, and animals in Africa and South America, noting that their distribution is hard to explain unless the two continents were once connected.

The problem was, however, that Wegener couldn't prove *how* the continents were forced apart or could move horizontally. In fact, it would not be until the 1940s and later, long after his death, that the technology would be invented that could detect the evidence that would eventually support his theory. As I was growing up, scientists were continuing to piece the evidence together that would finally change our ideas of continent formation and vindicate Wegener's proposal once and for all.

It was the developing theory of plate tectonics that most dramatically got my attention about the changeability of scientific theory, yet every branch of science can tell the same sorts of stories. Yesterday's certainty is today's nonsense, and vice versa.

Nonscientists often believe that any theory or hypothesis presented by scientists is true. However, any scientific theory is only what our scientists understand *today*. Tomorrow's discoveries could very well change everything. The fact is, as much as we have discovered, we still know very little about most things.

Since many of us are walking around with the scientific explanation of "what we are" embedded in our brains, let's take a closer look at this definition, its limitations, and how it ultimately fails.

2

Dividing the Universal Pie

The classification system most people learn in school divides our universe into two major categories—the physical, or nonliving, world and the biological, or living, world. The physical world is known as the mineral kingdom. The biological world has traditionally been subdivided into two kingdoms: the animal and vegetable kingdoms.* These kingdoms are then further subdivided into smaller and smaller groups according to narrowing physical criteria—division (for plants) or phylum (for animals), followed by subphylum, class, order, family, genus, and species.

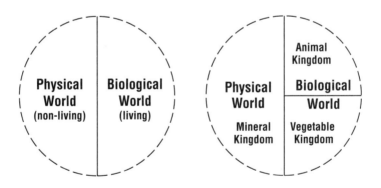

You, for example, belong to the kingdom *Animalia,* to which all animals belong. The phylum you belong to is *Chordata.* All creatures in this phylum

---

* Charts are for illustrative purposes only and do not represent percentages.

have—at some point in their lives—gills, a notocord (a flexible, rodlike cord that runs down the back of the body), and a hollow nerve tube that runs above the notocord. In addition, their bodies have right and left sides that are roughly alike. Many animals such as fish, amphibians, reptiles, birds, and mammals belong to this phylum. Some animals that don't belong to this phylum are mollusks, insects, jellyfish, and starfish.

Membership in the subphylum *Vertebrata* requires you to have a backbone and a brain case. Further subdivision puts you in the class *Mammalia*. This means you belong to a class of animals that feeds its young with mother's milk, has skin and hair, a skeleton, and an internal organ system.

So far, you are defined similarly to dogs and cats. Of course, while you share some features with them, there are also some dramatic differences between you and them. We part ways with our feline and canine brethren at the order *Primates*. To qualify for membership in this order, to which approximately 180 species belong, a species must have hands with five fingers and feet with five toes. Chimpanzees, gorillas, lemurs, and monkeys are some fellow primates.

We then divide further, to the family *Hominidae*, which consists solely of gorillas, chimpanzees, orangutans, bonobos, and human beings. Members of this family share an erect posture, a rounded skull with a large brain, small teeth, and are able to walk on two feet. Within this family are two subfamilies, one of which is called *Homininae* and consists of humans and African great apes.

The divisions aren't over yet! We are then divided into tribes—ours being *Hominini*, which includes modern human beings as well as extinct species such as *Australopithecus*, *Neanderthals*, and *Homo erectus*.

Human beings are the only living members of the *Hominini* tribe, which when divided further yields the genus *Homo*. Members of *Homo* have a well-developed opposable thumb, a hand that can grip with power and precision, and the ability to make standardized tools (most noteworthy is the ability to create one tool to make another tool).

The members of the species *sapiens* are further defined as having an approximately 1,350 cubic-centimeter brain capacity, a high forehead, small teeth and jaw, a well-defined chin, and the ability to make use of symbols, such as those used in writing and language. In fact, we are not just the species *Homo sapiens*, but the subspecies *Homo sapiens sapiens*. There has even been yet another fossil discovery in Africa that has been labeled *Homo sapiens idaltu* and is considered to be one of our own ancestors.

This system of classification, called taxonomy, was devised relatively recently. In fact, we have a long history of authoring a variety of systems that have influenced how people of the past have understood the world and their place in it. If you had been a student of Hippocrates, the "father of medicine," who lived around 400 B.C., you would have learned that the living world is composed of the four humors—blood, yellow bile, black bile, and phlegm—and that all disease results from the humors being out of balance. Had you been a student of Aristotle (a contemporary of Hippocrates), you would have learned that all living things could be divided into two groups—those with blood and those without. As a student of St. Augustine, the fourth-century Christian bishop and philosopher, you would have learned to classify animals according to whether they were found to be useful, harmful, or superfluous. If you had been an herbalist in the Middle Ages, you would have organized plants by what they produce, such as fruits, vegetables, or wood fibers.

It was not until the eighteenth century that Swedish biologist Carl von Linné established a system for classifying plants and animals according to their structural similarities. Modern taxonomy traces its roots to Linné's system, and over time, as knowledge increased, the subdivisions we are now familiar with became established and endured. Yet even this system of classification does not adequately describe the world.

Recently biologists have begun to divide the biological world into three kingdoms. Instead of using only the traditional animal and vegetable, they now propose to add a third kingdom—Protista—that is made up of those organisms that are not clearly animal or vegetable. A compelling example of such an organism is the single-cell euglena, which swims about like an animal with its whiplike flagella in search of food, has an eyespot that allows it to orient toward light, but contains bright green chloroplasts that allow it to perform photosynthesis like a plant.

Advancements in the fields of microbiology and biochemistry have increased our knowledge of the construction of cells and how they work. Scientists are finding that cells have more in common, as well as more differences, than was previously suspected. To address this, a five-kingdom classification system is now becoming more widely accepted. This system divides the living world into *Monera* (single cells without a nucleus—that is, bacteria), *Protoctista* (eukaryotic microorganisms, algae, water molds, slime molds and slime nets, and protozoa), *Fungi* (mushrooms, molds, and lichens), *Plantaea* (mosses, ferns, cone-bearing plants, and flowering plants), and *Animalia* (animals).

As we can see, the construction of any sort of model is a tenuous endeavor and is only a measure of what we understand. It does not tell us what actually is real.

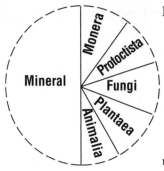

Even within the scientific community, there is disagreement as to how best to classify and categorize the universe.

This disagreement generally reflects specialized areas of study. For example, one scientist has proposed to categorize organisms according to patterns of larval development, while another believes it more accurate to base categorization on the linear order of amino acids that compose proteins.[1] If you understand the criteria I just mentioned, I salute you—clearly these criteria are very specialty specific and will most likely have great meaning only to the author and his or her scientific peers.

No matter how the sciences squabble over classifications, one thing remains the same. We are still left with the image of the human being as a big-headed, chin-jutting, letter-writing, tool-making animal that moves about on two feet. We are presented as one object among many, one slice out of the universal pie.

This description of the human being reflects the bias that all scientific models have in common—they are object-oriented and focus on the physical aspect of organisms. Although scientists

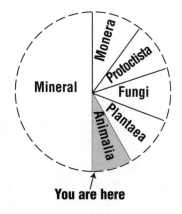

You are here

endeavor faithfully to unlock the secrets of the universe, a strictly object-oriented approach ignores intangible qualities that defy measurement and quantification. Thus the explanations resulting from such an approach are inherently incomplete.

For example, you have the power of thought, yet, scientifically speaking, those thoughts cannot be proven to exist. Some scientists believe that thoughts are simply chemical activities and the firing of neurons in the brain, and some maintain that thoughts do not exist at all. Should this throw the existence of your ability to think into doubt? Or should it merely highlight the obvious limitations of scientific inquiry?

Regardless of what anyone else says, our thoughts are a very real part of ourselves. Our thoughts get us up in the morning, moving on our two feet, and going about the business of making and using all these myriad tools that take us through each day. Nevertheless, this big part of who we are cannot be scientifically proven to exist.

We live in a universe that is not merely a collection of objects, it is a universe of processes as well. Stars are born and die, planets are formed, species evolve, ice ages come and go, eggs are fertilized, cells metabolize, trees grow and bear fruit, rain falls, passions are aroused, poetry is written. None of these processes happens in a vacuum. Processes act in relation to other processes.

In addition to powers and processes, *potential* is still another immeasurable quality. Carbon atoms have the potential to form both graphite, one of the softest minerals in the world, and diamond, one of the hardest. A newly hatched bird has the potential to fly. An acorn has the potential to become an oak tree. A tadpole has the potential to become a frog. You have all sorts of potential (to be discussed further), most of it still unrealized.

In the chapters that follow, we will consider these capacities and powers in order to build a new model—one that I believe presents a more satisfying and accurate picture of the universe. This new model will illustrate your place in the scheme of things and answer the question, *What am I?* In addition, it will shed light on the purpose of your existence and answer the question, *Why am I?* Finally, it will clarify your potential and answer the question, *What am I becoming?*

3

A New Model

Despite a good education that covered many branches of science, including the earth sciences, biology, and chemistry, I reached adulthood with a very sketchy map of how the universe was put together. I'd gotten to know some subjects very well (those areas I was most interested in), others moderately, and others hardly at all. For example, just the word *physics* scared me. Let's face it, the universe is a big place, and there's a lot to learn. I basically saw it as a conglomeration of objects—stars, planets, atoms, molecules, plants, and animals—where events happened, like supernovas, volcanic eruptions, floods, birth, and death.

Had I drawn a map of the universe as I understood it, it would have consisted of lots of galaxies. I'd have focused my attention on the Milky Way galaxy, and then the Sun and our solar system. Then I'd have zeroed in on Earth and shown it populated with a variety of plants and animals. Maybe I'd have drawn a stick figure of myself in the New England area of North America, waving and saying, "You are here." In my twenties I saw a T-shirt with a picture of the Milky Way galaxy and an arrow pointing to an outer arm saying exactly this: *You Are Here.* I found this perspective unique, and the truth of it made me laugh. Sometime later I bought and framed a star chart titled "Map of the Universe"—which still hangs in my office—to remind myself of my place in the scheme of things. When my life became too crazy, I would look at it and remind myself that all my personal affairs were mere flickers in comparison to the imponderable vastness of the universe.

And then, one day in my early thirties, I bought a book that would change how I regarded the universe and my place in it. I wasn't looking to change my perspective, and the book took me by surprise. The book is called *The Promulga-*

tion of Universal Peace, and it is a record of 'Abdu'l-Bahá's* talks given during his visit to the United States and Canada in 1912. I had already developed a great appreciation for 'Abdu'l-Bahá. His writings and talks about every subject of human concern are both the most rational and spiritual I have ever read, and he has the ability to make difficult concepts clear and simple.

I remember liking the weight and feel of that book. I felt excited to have it in my hands, and I couldn't wait to crack its binding and explore its contents. I opened the book at random, and one of the first things I came across was this:

All existing phenomena may be resolved into grades or kingdoms, classified progressively as mineral, vegetable, animal and human, each of which possesses its degree of function and intelligence. When we consider the mineral, we find that it exists and is possessed of the power of affinity or combination. The vegetable possesses the qualities of the mineral plus the augmentative virtue or power of growth. It is, therefore, evident that the vegetable kingdom is superior to the mineral. The animal kingdom in turn possesses the qualities of the mineral and vegetable plus the five senses of perception whereof the kingdoms below it are lacking. Likewise, the power of memory inherent in the animal does not exist in the lower kingdoms.

Just as the animal is more noble than the vegetable and mineral, so man is superior to the animal. . . . Man is possessed of the emanations of consciousness; he has perception, ideality and is capable of discovering the mysteries of the universe. All the industries, inventions and facilities surrounding our daily life were at one time hidden secrets of nature, but the reality of man penetrated them and made them subject to his purposes. According to nature's laws they should have remained latent and hidden; but man, having transcended those laws, discovered these mysteries and brought them out of the plane of the invisible into the realm of the known and visible. How wonderful is the spirit of man![1]

I had never before heard the world described in such a way, not as a collection of objects at all, but as powers and qualities. With very few words 'Abdu'l-Bahá had changed my entire concept of the universe and set my future course of study.

---

* 'Abdu'l-Bahá is the son and appointed successor of Bahá'u'lláh.

I felt the need to really explore this model and to read up further on the sciences, to dive into the details and see if there was any conflict between the scientific models and 'Abdu'l-Bahá's description. I began where 'Abdu'l-Bahá began and drew a circle to represent the mineral kingdom and its inherent power of *attraction*.

Physicists are hard at work trying to discover the most fundamental unit of matter. At present, the most basic units of matter are believed to be the lepton and quark. Theories differ as to the construction of the lepton and quark. According to the Standard Model of particle physics, they are zero-dimensional, having no internal structure or size, while the promising String Theory defines leptons and quarks as one-dimensional strings whose mass and charge are determined by how the string vibrates.[2]

Whatever their true natures, quarks combine to form neutrons and protons. The electron—a lepton and a fundamental particle in its own right—combines with neutrons and protons to form atoms. Atoms combine to form molecules, and molecules combine to form minerals. Throughout this great dance of mixing and matching, attraction is the overarching principle.

In addition to the attribute of attraction, the vegetable kingdom manifests the power of *augmentation*, or growth.

Augmentative powers are recognized through many activities, such as the absorption and metabolization of nutrients, growth, and reproduction.

At the vegetable level, the cell makes its appearance. The power of growth is demonstrated in ever-increasing complexity, from the most simple single-cell creatures (cells without a nucleus), to more complex single cells (cells with a nucleus), to colonial cells (such as algae), to fungi, and finally, to the most complex organisms of the vegetable level, trees and plants. The variety with which the members of this kingdom live and reproduce is astounding, yet each member possesses the attribute of augmentation.

In addition to attraction and augmentation, the animal kingdom displays the power to *perceive* the surrounding environment. This power of perception is accompanied by the attributes of *intelligence* and *emotion*. The members of this kingdom act in response to what they perceive, and the degrees of animal existence can range from those creatures almost purely driven by instinct, such as the hornet, to those that display great intelligence and creativity along with a wide emotional repertoire, such as chimpanzees.

When we reach the next kingdom, a little observation uncovers powers that are distinctly human. Unlike animals, humans can think ahead, planning and working for the distant future. We even think about what lies beyond this physical life—about what happens after death. Even those who believe nothing happens after death can conceive of a time "after death."

We are wonderers, pondering the questions of "Who am I?" "Where did I come from?" and "Where am I going?" Granted, we ponder these questions in differing degrees, with some giving the questions intense thought and others giving them very little of their time. As a result, we come to a variety of conclusions about our identities, our origins, and our futures.

Humans can also change their minds and decide that what they previously considered true is actually untrue or needs to be modified as the result of new experiences or information. We are always revising our opinions and beliefs, and we can also change our own behavior. We can sometimes even break our own habits—often through great effort—and form new behavior patterns.

Furthermore, we can willingly sacrifice the most basic necessities of life, such as food or shelter, for an abstract principle. We can even sacrifice our most vital resource—our life itself—in the name of an abstract cause. Thus soldiers sacrifice themselves in the name of patriotism, and martyrs choose to allow themselves to be killed for their religious convictions.

We can also make decisions of an abstract nature, such as weighing moral choices. When we make such a choice, the concepts of right or wrong are vital aspects of that choice. We can choose how to act and not simply respond emotionally. For example, I may become annoyed with another person, but I can strive for patience and speak with tact despite having the urge to strike out or speak sharply. In fact, humans have a broad spectrum of moral behaviors to choose from that can allow us to act differently from what our emotions urge us to do.

Additionally, a human being is not a prisoner to instinct or the laws of nature. Although the animal, vegetable, and mineral kingdoms must comply with natural laws, human beings are not bound by their physical limitations and are not dominated by instinct. For example, humans can fly without wings and swim without gills. We can even defy gravity, leave our own planet, and live in places that would otherwise be impossible to live in were we constrained by the laws of nature.

**

Let's look at the picture we have been constructing. This model differs from the scientific model in that it stops carving up the universe like some kind of big pie and instead organizes it into concentric circles.

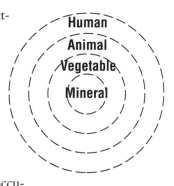

This approach allows us to see that each kingdom exhibits the powers of the kingdoms it encompasses, along with additional powers and capacities. For example, occupants of the mineral kingdom do not have augmentative powers, and occupants of the vegetable kingdom have both the powers of attraction and augmentation but do not possess perceptive powers, intelligence, or emotions.

In addition, this model illustrates the intimate interrelation between kingdoms. The vegetable power of augmentation could not exist without the mineral power of attraction, and the animal powers of intelligence, perception, and emotion could not manifest themselves without the powers of both attraction and augmentation. Similarly, human powers could not be made manifest without the powers of the mineral, vegetable, and animal kingdoms.

However much improvement this concentric model may represent over the taxonomic model, I was dismayed to find it still inadequate to the task of categorizing certain organisms. For example, I was not sure where to place the virus, which is merely a strand of DNA or RNA in a protein coat. It exists in a crystalline mineral state until it makes contact with its host cell, where it comes to life and begins to reproduce itself. Should I place the virus in the mineral or vegetable kingdom? It can reproduce, after all, although not without help from the vegetable and animal worlds. But that is all it does. It doesn't eat, and it doesn't metabolize.

Trying to categorize a virus is just one example of the inadequacy of the concentric model. I found myself plagued by a plethora of other creatures with strange precursors to the senses, and this frustrated my attempts to label them as either animal or vegetable. My first impulse was to force these aberrant creatures (well, inconvenient, at any rate) into this model anyway. Yet that would destroy my original intent to develop a model that accurately portrays reality. Still, I know I can't scrap the whole thing, for this model does, at least, convey the powers and capacities that exist in the world.

In the end, I discover that one slight modification transforms my concentric circles into a model capable of including all, a model that is also a symbol we encounter repeatedly around the world and throughout history. This slight, yet vital, modification gives us a new model and reintroduces a very ancient symbol—the spiral.

Take a moment to contemplate the spiral. This symbol indicates motion and development, process and unfoldment. Deceptively simple and yet undeniably complex, the spiral offers a unique picture and means of categorization. Although there is a starting point in the center, one gets the impression that it is not the real starting point but rather the point at which things become discernible. The open end of the spiral indicates that something could very well lie beyond our reach in the other direction.

I am reminded of the Doppler effect, which is experienced when a swiftly moving object passes by. Think of the sound of a motorcycle rushing past you. Out of silence, you first notice the almost inaudible high-pitched sound of its engine. The pitch drops, and the sound grows louder as the motorcycle moves toward you. The motorcycle passes swiftly by, and its pitch and volume continue to drop until you can no longer hear it.

You know that the motorcycle did not come into being when you heard it, and neither did it wink out of existence when you could no longer hear it. The spiral represents the same idea. The world does not come into existence at the starting point of the spiral, and neither does it dissolve out of existence at the endpoint. The beginning and end of this model simply represent the limits of what we can observe.

By tracing the spiral, one can conceive how, from the observable starting point of attraction, augmentation gradually appears, followed by perception and intelligence, and followed again by our own human attributes. No sudden leaps are required in this model. Instead, we find continuous, uninterrupted evolution and development, unfolding potential, and ongoing processes. There is a place for everyone in this model.

The spiral can be used to demonstrate many processes large and small. It can be used to portray the evolution of life on this planet, and it can be used to portray your own individual development. We will be referring to this symbol often as we proceed further with our explorations.

***

Let's use the spiral with a slight variation to demonstrate the interrelatedness of all things. Instead of showing the capabilities of different organisms, the diagram on the following page shows the results of those capabilities. In this diagram, we start with the quark and lepton. Quarks combine to form protons and neutrons, which in turn combine with electrons to form atoms. Atoms bond with other atoms to form molecules, especially complex macromolecules, such as enzymes, proteins, and amino acids. Macromolecules combine to form cells, cells combine to form tissues, tissues combine to form organs, and organs combine to form an organism.

Organisms are attracted to other organisms and often form permanent social groups, such as herds of wildebeests or schools of fish. At the next level, the ecoweb emerges, which is the interdependence of creatures within a certain area. In a simplified version of an ecoweb, we might find within a given area foxes and lynxes feeding upon rabbits and field mice. The rabbits and field mice, in turn, feed on the local vegetation. The vegetation absorbs nutrients from the soil, which has been enriched by the decomposition of all the ecoweb's organisms. These organisms, in turn, are broken down through the activities of insects and bacteria. In an ecoweb, therefore, the viability of a system depends on all its members.

After the stage of the organism, we reach the level of humans, and we find humans creating families, who come together to form communities. Communities, in turn, gather to form states, states combine to form nations, and nations form a global federation (to which the embryonic United Nations currently serves as a precursor). At this global level—and we are only now learning this—we

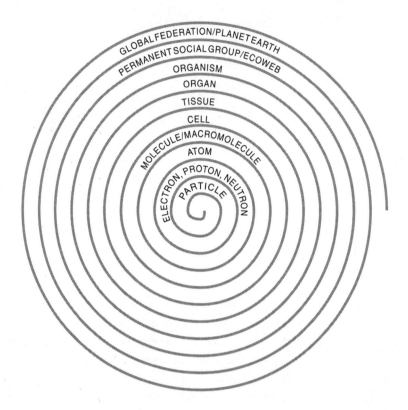

can see that the whole planet is actually one interdependent system and that any event that occurs on one part of the globe can seriously affect all the other parts. For example, in 1815, Mt. Tambora, a volcano on a small island in the South Pacific, erupted. One of the most powerful volcanic eruptions in history, the explosion caused global cooling and erratic weather patterns that are now blamed for droughts and resulting famines that followed shortly after in Europe.[3] We also know that the South American rain forest does much of the "breathing" for the planet, helping to clean the air and greatly contributing to the world's supply of oxygen. That region's deforestation is now the subject of much concern as scientists debate the effect this will have on our planet's overall ecological health.

The process of categorization extends even beyond our own planet. We know, for example, that the Earth is part of the solar system. Our solar system, in turn, belongs to a galaxy of stars called the Milky Way, and our Milky Way belongs to a group of galaxies known as the Local Group. And the categories, I must assume, continue on and on, to even higher levels. Exploring and understanding the interconnectedness of all these systems is something we must leave to future generations. Still, we can appreciate the pattern we are beginning to observe, a pattern that illustrates the intrinsic interconnectedness and interdependence of all things. No matter what the level of organization is, each living being belongs and contributes to the existence and functioning of a much vaster realm than its own.

4

Worlds Apart

Sitting atop the rocky overlook, I survey Somes Sound below and watch the yachts and pleasure boats leaving white frothy paths behind them in the water. From here, I have a view of summer mansions on the opposite shore, with their private docks stretching out into the water.

Below me stretches a closely manicured lawn. On this spot, French Jesuits had established a mission in 1613, only to see it destroyed in short order by the English. For such a small island Maine's Mt. Desert Island certainly has a rich history. First inhabited by the indigenous Abenaki, then colonized and fought over by the French and English, it is now a vacation getaway for middle class and ultra-rich alike.

It has been a satisfying hike so far, with the song of the wood thrush accompanying me for a good part of it—sometimes frustratingly near, but always remaining out of sight. I notice a dark form gliding below me over the lawn and raise my binoculars. It is a hawk—perhaps it is looking for lunch? I won't eat my own lunch until I reach the rocky shore below, but a snack might be in order, and I'm in no hurry to leave this spot.

I find a rock worn smooth by glaciers and subsequent millennia of rain—now deliciously warmed by the sun—and lean back. The heat seeps into my back muscles. Oh, rock, that feels so good, thank you. And sun, thank you for warming this rock. Thank you, wind, for cooling me off. Thank you, God, for the fine weather, the safe drive to one of my favorite places, and this feeling of well-being. I can't seem to send my gratitude in enough directions. Now that I'm here, I realize how much I needed this time, immersed in nature and away from my daily routine, in order to slow down and recover some sense of balance.

It is too obvious to me, at this moment, that my life has become a stream of "to-dos," one task after another that demands I take no rest until they are all done. Well, for today, the to-do list has been left behind, along with my increasingly short temper. It's a simple reality that when I don't spend time in the woods—at least once a week—the world begins to drive me crazy. Little irritants become big irritants, and there gradually develops a pesky undercurrent of anxiety and agitation. Endless commitments and responsibilities induce a type of amnesia—I forget both my need for nature, and that anxiety is a sign that I am out of balance. When I finally get back into the woods, I realize, as if for the first time, how vital it is for me to spend time immersed in a natural setting. At this moment, I am feeling quite myself again. A burden seems to be literally lifted from my shoulders.

I continue to watch the hawk on its patrol. I have heard that in some Native American cultures the hawk is considered a messenger. Do you bring me a message, hawk? The hawk, flying so high, sees the broad view. Watching it, I am reminded that I need to broaden my own vision. I have become so overwhelmed by the details of everyday life that I've forgotten to look at the big picture. Maybe it's time to take a look at my own life, time to set some new goals, time to cast off certain parts of my life that don't work for me anymore.

I close my eyes, feeling the breeze play with my hair. After a while, my mind begins to wander, the way it does when I allow myself to slow down and become still. I realize that I am in a unique position here. I am appreciating the warmth and smoothness of this rock I lean against, whereas the rock itself has no idea it is being leaned on or that the concept of *appreciation* even exists. Nor does it have any concept of the sun or that it is being warmed by it. Rocks form, and rocks dissolve. This rock that I am addressing as an individual is actually an outcropping of a much larger formation that composes this mountain and its neighbors. As a member of the mineral degree of existence, it is quite oblivious to the life that has taken hold of it.

On this hike, I have passed ferns, mosses, trillium, white pine, aspen, balsam, and so much more. All these have found a foothold on this mountain and have thrived. They take up the nutrients and water from the soil, growing, reproducing, and covering this mountain with forest. This rock may have no knowledge of me, but what about the green growing things I passed as I made my way up the mountain? Were they aware that I walked beneath the leafy green canopy, inhaling the sweet fresh air, its rich blend of balsam and earth, as if these are the most precious of fragrances? I think not. But certainly all these green plants know something of the sun, for their life cycles are synchronized with the passing seasons, the lengthening days, and the increased sunlight. The photosynthesis these plants perform is only possible with sunlight. But while I can call the plant world *dependent* on the sun, I don't think I can call it *aware*.

I consider the animals I encountered as I hiked. I had heard the warning trill of numerous squirrels that were definitely aware of me and made sure everybody else became aware, too. The chipmunks that darted in and out of the stone wall would eventually find the small deposit of sunflower seeds I left. They, too, had been aware of me. The chickadees knew I was there, too, but they had seemed indifferent to my presence. The mosquitoes and black flies even now know I'm here, and how I wish they didn't.

I know this mountain forest is full of animals, some I'll never see because I've never learned to step softly enough to avoid detection. All of them utilize the mineral and vegetable worlds that make up the forest. They all depend on water. Trees are not only sources of food but places to build nests, both in the branches and in the trunks. Even stone walls are utilized for this purpose. Squirrels and chipmunks can become food for predators, so they had better be aware. The animals that stalk them—foxes and the like—are not only fast but smart and intent on success.

Yet, for all this awareness and intelligence, those creatures are barred from what goes on in the mind of this woman who rests now on their mountain. They don't know her motivation for leaving the sunflower seeds nor her satisfaction as she takes in the view of the sound below. They will never be privy to the symbolic meaning she has assigned to the hawk nor the chain of thought that is presently going on in her mind. Her private prayer of thanks is quite removed from their sphere. They may hear it as a sigh that escapes her, a quiet whisper, but they cannot know its intent, its content, or its meaning.

Can the same be said about me? Are there things that I am as oblivious to as the rock is to me, as the squirrel is to the efforts I make on my life's journey? Do these circles within circles continue past and beyond me? Does this spiral continue on to a place, a condition, a level of existence of which I am completely unaware? Are there more levels, with dimensions as foreign to me as my prayer is to this rock? In other words, could there be kingdoms, degrees of existence, beyond ours?

I can't actually answer these questions, because at this point I come up against an impenetrable barrier—my own human limitations. I can only picture that which can be seen, heard, smelled, tasted, and felt. If there are planes of existence higher than the human plane, it could very well be made up of things that can't be seen, heard, smelled, tasted, or felt. Perhaps I can imagine the reality of such a degree of existence, but I cannot confirm it with my senses.

I recall a thought experiment I came up with some years ago, which I call the "cinnamon whistle experiment." I imagine a whistle made of cinnamon candy and picture the smooth texture of the whistle with its deep crimson color. I imagine the tangy smell of cinnamon and visualize putting the whistle to my lips and tasting its spicy flavor. Then I blow the whistle and listen to the shrill sound it makes.

Now I imagine I have lost my eyesight and can no longer see the whistle. Of course I can still hear it, smell its pungent aroma, feel its smooth surface, and taste its sweetness. Now I imagine I have lost my hearing. Still, I can feel, smell, and taste the whistle. Only now I imagine that I have lost my sense of taste and smell. All I can do at this point is feel the whistle. According to this tragic line of events, however, I now imagine that I have lost my sense of touch and cannot even feel the whistle.

In this scenario, I can no longer feel the whistle, taste it, smell it, hear it, or see it. The question is, does the whistle no longer exist? If I had no senses at all, would the world cease to exist? Obviously not. The reason I can't perceive the whistle has everything to do with me and nothing to do with the whistle. Just because I can't sense a thing doesn't mean it doesn't exist. Imagine a world that cannot be perceived by the senses—can anything be imagined at all?

This experiment helped me realize that the ability to perceive a thing is not a factor in whether or not that thing exists. I already know this, really. I know that infrared and ultraviolet light exist, although I can't observe either directly. I know that X-rays exist but cannot see X-rays myself. I know that elephants communicate over vast distances using calls of a frequency so low I cannot hear them. I know that bats emit a high-pitched call that allows them to locate their prey. However, I can't hear that call myself.

These are phenomena that occur within the physical sphere of existence, yet I need assistance to detect their presence. Of course, these things belong to that which I can perceive, both light and sound. What about something that exists in realms of existence that encompass ours? I may have as much chance of comprehending or perceiving those phenomena as a plant has of comprehending thought or perceiving a great work of art.

Just as the unconsciousness of the plant cannot disprove the existence of human consciousness, neither do my own perceptual limitations disprove the existence of an encompassing reality.

As I continue my journey down this mountain, toward the rocky shore where I will finally eat my sandwich, I feel less alone. I feel *encompassed.* I am too well aware of my own limitations to assume that what I know, and all there is to know, are confined to that which my brain and senses perceive. It simply isn't logical.

5

Human Development

The Physical Stage

Up to this point we have been talking about the world in general. I have described the environment in which every human being finds himself or herself. Together we have taken a fresh look at the world in which we find ourselves, redefining the world in terms of powers and attributes rather than physical characteristics.

Now it's time to get personal. What can the spiral teach us about human development—not as a species, but as individuals?

I sit for long moments, pen poised above paper. I know I did not spontaneously appear here, with this pen held so comfortably in my hand ready to record my thoughts on a piece of lined paper. I arrived here through a long process of development, a process that began long before I uttered my first word, before I could hold a pen, before I could outline my first letter.

I spiral back, tracing the roots of this moment to the very beginning, to when two pieces of DNA, the genetic material contributed by my father and mother, combined forces.

This is a somewhat unnerving thought. How could all these thoughts, all of what I am at this moment, have started with two bits of material so tiny and negligible? How could it be that when these two bits joined forces, there was none to notice and mark it as an Event of Consequence (at least for me)? How could something so far removed from consciousness result in this body, this life, and, in fact, consciousness itself?

It seems strange, thinking about it now, that two tiny strands of genetic material, existing in their separate universes of two independent bodies, would actually be given the opportunity to meet. But there were greater forces at work that would propel those two genetic bits toward a rendezvous. Or, as my father used to say, "Men and women have always found ways to get together."

Until then, those two distinct bundles of chromosomes hovered in a narrow space of opportunity between the mineral and vegetable worlds. Each had the potential to enter the world of biological processes. Yet, without the requisite merger, each would have continued to exist within the confines of mineral limitations.

On the day that my mother's egg allowed a particular sperm to penetrate, an amazing thing happened, for that conjugation instantly catapulted two denizens of the mineral kingdom into the vegetable kingdom. For shortly after the merger, the fertilized egg divided into two cells, then four, and then eight. In short, a higher condition of existence was instantaneously achieved.

Yet something more incredible was achieved in that instant, something hidden behind the hoopla of all that furious cell division. For in that moment *I* came into being. What we might observe in the moment is the frenzy of mitosis, and this itself is an arresting spectacle. But hidden within all that biological activity was the potential for this moment, as I wait with pen in hand to capture thoughts about life's meaning as they surface.

This potential belongs to only one species out of the numerous species that inhabit this planet. For the acorn certainly does not possess this potential. Rather, it holds within it the potential to grow, to absorb water and nutrients through its roots, and to use sunlight to fuel its biological processes. It has the potential to produce more acorns.

Given enough lessons, a member of our closest biological kin, the chimpanzees, might learn how to hold a pen, but from that pen only meaningless scribbles would be produced. The chimpanzee will never be able to produce the repeating symbols necessary to convey thoughts about the purpose of existence.

When I was first conceived, I was no more impressive than a newly pollinated oak flower or a newly conceived chimpanzee. Set the rapidly dividing cells of these three microscopic dots—the flower, the chimpanzee, and me—side by side. Taken at face value, they appear to be equivalent. Only by following their respective developmental paths do we find that their very distinct ends are contained in their beginnings. In my case, as with every human being, that end involves capacities such as abstract thought, language, and the use of symbols.

Taking a second look at that moment of conception, I find the event gives me something profound to reflect upon. In order to achieve the elevation of the chromosomes from the mineral to the vegetable world, the individual identities of the egg and sperm had to be sacrificed. One had to give up its identity as an egg and the other its identity as a sperm in order to move into the higher realm of vegetable activity. What captivates me is this idea of "sacrifice," a term that is generally associated with cruelty (the virgin was taken to the sacrificial altar) or nobility (he sacrificed himself on the field of battle), and definitely with death. Sacrifice is also a concept found in many religious traditions as a necessary component for spiritual transformation. Thus people fast or curb their various appetites in the hope of advancing spiritually. I can only feel awe to witness how this sacrifice at conception also works—and that it does indeed work—at a purely biological level.

But looking at it in another way, the egg and sperm were not sacrificed during fertilization but *transformed* into something greater. It was not annihilation; it was a dramatic and fundamental change in their natures. Those chromosomes still existed, yet when they united, the qualities of eggness and spermness disappeared forever. In their place appeared something exponentially greater.

At conception, I immediately attained the powers of augmentation, a sign that I had reached the higher, vegetable level of existence. By the time I was implanted in the wall of my mother's womb, my cells were rapidly dividing, and I was absorbing nutrients and growing. After only eight days, I was comprised of about two hundred cells, almost every one of which was different from the other. Those two hundred cells would become my heart, brain, liver, skin, and all the vital organs that support my biological processes.

And here I pause again to consider yet another strange thing. Although this original transformative unification of two strands of chromosomes has produced a diversification of comparatively dizzying dimensions, those diverse cells cannot go their separate ways. They are destined to work in conjunction with one another and are inexorably bound together. Distinct yet unified, each has a vital contribution to make to the overall functioning of this growing organism.

As soon as there were enough cells, the entire bundle folded in half. The groove between the two folds then closed to form a neural tube, and one end began to swell.

I had only been in the world for three weeks, yet signs of future greatness were already being advertised—that little swelling was the beginning of my brain. Nerves from my brain stem began to develop, as did my backbone. Around my brain my head then developed with a gaping opening, which was destined to become my mouth. Soon after this, my embryonic heart developed and began to beat.

And here, so soon again, I experienced another momentous turn of events—the appearance of my nervous system. That forming network of nerves, primitive as it was, was leading me toward the greater world of the animal. At this stage I am reminded of the flatworm, with its simple nervous system that lets it detect chemical changes. A little later, my nervous system would resemble that of the jellyfish, which responds to touch. But this was just the beginning for me, and I only use those two examples for convenient comparison. It wouldn't take long for my nervous system to exceed them both.

Given another week of growth—a total of four now—my face and head were just becoming distinguishable. Four tiny bumps were just beginning to sprout where my arms and legs would grow. Thyroid gland, lungs, liver, pancreas, and kidneys were all in the works. Pretty impressive for something the size of a small pea!

My environment was assisting my development in some key ways. Whenever I made contact with any surface, impulses traveled along my growing nervous system. Specific cells in my developing brain then received those impulses and became permanently responsible for specific information. One group of brain cells would receive information from the left foot, another group from the right hand. This continuous interaction with my environment helped shape and perfect me.

As my nascent ears and brain formed, different sounds became increasingly perceptible, such as my mother's heartbeat, my own heartbeat, and the gurgling sounds of food being digested. My mother's voice became a part of my aural environment, muffled and indistinct. Now and then something unusual might intrude—the BANG of a firecracker, perhaps. Far from suggesting to me the existence of a world greater than my own, these sounds simply served to strengthen the neural connections between my ears and brain. Nevertheless, unconscious as I was of this greater world, I was already being influenced by it and already belonged to it.

During my time in the womb, my predominant condition might be thought of as *vegetable*. After all, most of my time was spent growing and absorbing nutrients. Yet everything that was growing was ushering me beyond a vegetative existence. My brain, nervous system, and sensory organs, even as they developed, were building bridges between myself and the rest of the world. Indeed, the whole point of these vegetable processes was to enable the development of the animal powers of perception, intelligence, and emotion. Those very few stimuli offered in the womb were enough to prepare me for the greater stimuli that would come when I left the womb.

Each day it became ever more apparent that all this biological activity was taking me beyond the limits of the vegetable world. My brain, very early on, had sent out two rudimentary stalks that would develop into eyes. Those stalks were certainly not necessary in the confined and dusky environment of the womb. Yet these, too, immediately sent impulses to my brain, developing and perfecting the system that would one day allow me to discern shapes, colors, depth, and motion. Eyes and ears, arms and legs—had I the power to wonder about them, I could not have conceived of the reason behind their existence. In fact, they had no purpose in the womb, but they were in the process of developing for a future time when they would provide information and respond to the directions of my developing brain. My digestive system was forming, passing amniotic fluid, and perfecting itself for the day when it would be required to digest food. Signals were passing back and forth between my brain and other organs, which were engaged in continuous preparation for the day I would be required to exist as an independently functioning individual.

What a busy time this was for me, yet how far I still had to go before that pen, which at the beginning of this section was left poised above paper, would become accessible. It hardly matters that an actual pen hovered regularly within inches of me, whenever my mother composed a letter, note, or grocery list. My whole world was confined to the vegetable world of biological processes, and the pen lay well beyond my own personal horizon.

Day by day I advanced ever closer to a pivotal event. My development was beginning to put a strain on my two most precious resources—food and space. My mother's body could not spare enough nutrients to fuel my growth much longer, and I was running out of room.

Finally, with my world quaking and shuddering around me, what was once my safe haven became eager to be rid of me. I might have considered that eviction cruelty itself, had I any notion of cruelty. Yet the cataclysmic event of my birth was a vital step in my development. It might not have been fun, but it was necessary.

What was it like for me? I can only imagine. Perhaps I felt enormous pressure from the uterine contractions. Things must have gone dark and quiet, with the sounds that had been amplified by the conductive amniotic fluid suddenly dampened. Then it was just me and waves of pressure, slowly increasing in intensity. I flowed with it. The contractions massaged my arms, my legs, my head, my chest.

45

I was motion. The world was motion. And then, poised between the world of the womb and the greater world beyond, all things slowed to a standstill. One more push, and the pressure was gone. I gasped reflexively and felt a strange raw feeling in my lungs as I inhaled my first breath of air.

Suddenly I found myself in a world of endless stimuli. Sounds were sharp, lights were bright. I was immediately bombarded with new sensations as the doctor examined me, as I was washed and wrapped in a soft blanket and put into my mother's arms. I heard my mother's voice, startlingly clear and near.

This squalling newborn, testing her lungs for the first time, bore no resemblance to what she was just nine short months ago. At that time, she had been a microscopic dot of dividing cells, and now here she was, seven pounds and four ounces, fists flailing, legs kicking, face screwed up, making a noise folks could hear down the hall.

And yet, what had changed for me from one day to the next? Yes, I had been rather dramatically thrust from my watery home to a new land of air and earth. Yes, the umbilical cord that had literally attached me to my mother had been severed. Still, I remained totally dependent on her for nourishment and protection, and I remained oblivious to the world that stretched out before me.

This was nothing more, in the scheme of things, than a passage—indeed a *critical* passage—into a new environment that would allow the next phase of development to begin.

6

Human Development

The Emotional and Cognitive Stage

The very first photo ever taken of me was as I exited the hospital where I was born. Actually, I'm not even visible in the photo. I am hidden in a bundle of blankets, cradled in the arms of a nurse who is smiling down at me. My mother is busy greeting my three older sisters, pulling two-year-old Susan toward her for a hug while four-year-old Kathy and three-year-old Diane crowd close around her, vying for their share of attention.

What was it like for me at that time? Was I aware of the cotton cap on my head, the diaper on my bottom, or the blanket I was wrapped in? Did I know the difference between the nurse who held me and my mother? Did I recognize the voices of my sisters, to whom I had been listening, albeit in a very muffled way, as my ears and brain developed? If the day was sunny and pleasant as I left the hospital, did I know it to be a very fine day? Did I anticipate meeting the family dog, Cindy, whose barking I had heard over these past few months? Was I aware of the photographer, my father, who was busy documenting this increase in his family circle?

I have often tried to imagine the world as the newborn experiences it. Research shows that a newborn can only focus between a distance of eight to ten inches.[1] I was born, in other words, legally blind. In fact, my body was so underdeveloped that the only thing I was good at was flailing my arms and legs. I did have certain reflexes that would help me along a bit, however. I could grasp, and I could suck. Thanks to the sucking reflex, I had already experienced my first taste sensation—the sweetness of milk. The day I left the hospital, I could only display two emotions: contentment and distress. Physical discomfort distressed me; physical comfort made me content.

There I was, basically immobile with nothing to do, not that it mattered. I had no desire to go anywhere or do anything. Indeed, I had no idea there was anywhere to go or anything to do. I didn't have a thought in my head or a desire in the world except, perhaps, to be warm, dry, and full. And even those were not things I thought about. They were just things I made a fuss about when they went missing.

I am tempted to compare that condition to a blank slate, just waiting to be written on by some outside hand. But an infant is no more a blank slate than an acorn is. An acorn has the potential to become an oak tree, while an infant has the potential to become an adult human being. Some of what I would become was inherited—my blue eyes, my brown hair, my height, or the way I laughed. Other things, however, might not be so apparently genetic. My love for reading is shared by the entire family. Does that mean it's genetic? However, I like a quiet life, while others in my family thrive in company. My personality, my temperament, my interests—there could be much debate about how much of this is inherited and how much is the result of the experiences my environment provides.

From my first moments, every sound, smell, and sensation would influence my development. From moment to moment I received a medley of stimulation: the roar of a car engine . . . the aroma of soup simmering on the stove . . . the fresh fragrance of my soft, newly washed blanket . . . the warmth of my father's broad hand on my back . . . the laughter of my sisters as they played hide and seek . . . my cold wet diaper being replaced by a dry one . . . the continuous parade of familiar and unfamiliar voices.

Incredibly complex physiological processes were at work in which brain cells made connection after connection as a result of all this stimulation. No one experiences his or her brain cells making those connections in any conscious way, of course. It is something that happens while we are doing other things and actually *because* we are doing other things.

A baby's brain can be compared to a sponge in some ways because it is affected and changed by all that it absorbs. But brain development is not determined simply by random stimulation. We are not shaped by the environment, only influenced by it. We are speaking of a *human* baby after all, and, while external stimulation *is* critical to its development, there are certain things a human being's brain will eventually be able to do, and certain things a human being's brain will never be able to do.

A baby learns, for example, to discern all the little sounds that compose a language, but she will never be able to discern the high-pitched sounds that bats make, no matter how many bats she is exposed to. However, a baby's brain is very flexible. The brain might be designed to acquire language, but languages vary enormously. A baby born in Japan will have a very different language experience than a baby born in England. Many of an infant's likes and dislikes will be determined by his or her culture, and a person raised on one kind of diet may later find foods from another culture unpalatable.

When I think about a newborn's perception of the world and look for some comparison, a before-and-after experience I've had as an adult that might help me understand an infant's experience, I remember the time I took it upon myself to learn to identify the local wildflowers. Until then, I only recognized a few distinguishing characteristics. Basically, flowers came in different colors—mostly orange, yellow, blue, and white. And those were the flowers I noticed. I soon discovered that there were many wildflowers I hadn't noticed at all. I began to find them in every environment, and as I studied each flower's unique features, as I learned to distinguish one from the other, a world of astounding diversity opened up for me.

Colors came in every hue. Yellow was no longer yellow. It became pale, or golden, or vivid. Orange became dusty, or bright, or reddish. Flowers weren't just shaped like the starbursts I had been drawing since childhood; they were shaped like birds, bells, spheres, and even sacs. Some were so tiny I needed a magnifying glass to get a good look at them. Flowers grew close to the ground, on vines, on bushes, and on stalks six feet high. They dangled like bells, crowned the stalk like a sunburst, or encircled the stem in whorls. Overall plant shapes differed widely. Even their foliage, previously a generic green, I learned to see anew—gray, yellow, brown, blue, with leaf shapes varying from flat and wide to light and feathery and everything in between.

Is it this way for the newborn? Is smell just a generic sensation until we learn to distinguish one smell from another? Is the smell of simmering soup pretty much the same as the smell of newly cut grass? What about sound? Can a newborn hear the difference between an orchestra playing Vivaldi's *Four Seasons* and a barking dog? Or are such stimuli essentially meaningless to a newborn?

No matter how much of the world began as an indistinguishable sensory blur, this condition was only temporary. I soon learned the normal sounds of my home environment—like my sisters' voices, the vacuum cleaner, a television program, or Cindy barking. At that point, I did not think to myself, "That's Cindy barking." The repeated sound simply became a familiar part of my aural environment. It took me a couple of months to learn that certain things, such as being fed, happened at regular intervals. I also learned that when I cried, I would be picked up, fed, or otherwise comforted.

In just a few months, I had developed some very concrete expectations about my world. For example, I had learned to expect to be fed by my mother. Had someone else other than my mother one day appeared to feed me, I would certainly have been surprised. Or, if I were not fed as soon as I expected, I would have become frustrated and angry and voiced my displeasure with increasingly louder and dramatic wails.

Surprise and anger are signs that some type of mental process is at work, for in order to experience surprise or anger, a being must be intelligent. It is hard to surprise a butterfly, and yes, even hard to surprise a human newborn. A few months after birth, however, a baby is capable of showing surprise, while the butterfly never will.

These displays of surprise and anger were the first detectable signs that the next phase of my development—cognitive and emotional development—had begun. Emotion and cognition are inseparable components of intelligence. It is our intelligence that allows us to successfully navigate our environment and learn by experience. Through cognition, I learned the layout of our house. I learned about those things that posed a danger to me, such as a hot burner or an electrical outlet. My cognition made it possible for me to learn what to expect from my parents. And, in some ways more importantly, it helped me to learn what to expect from my sisters.

Older siblings are the behemoths of a child's personal world. A fourth child like myself is born into a situation of disadvantage. She is smaller, less experienced, and at the mercy of those who are not simply unsympathetic to her physical and mental inferiority but, in fact, are inclined to take advantage of them. My cognition would help me map out the complex and changeable social landscape of my family.

Emotion—that often-ignored dimension of intelligence—is that which *moves* us. Under normal circumstances we move toward things that we like and that make us happy, and we move away from things that we dislike or that scare us. If something doesn't evoke an emotion, we generally ignore it. Sometimes, when we act in self-defense this can work in reverse, and anger can cause us to face the very thing that scares us. For instance, I can remember a dog charging at me as I rode my bicycle down the street. Instead of trying to outpace the dog, I stopped and, with heart pounding, looked right at it and YELLED. I didn't think about it; my actions were automatic. It was only in retrospect that I wondered if it was the smartest thing to do. Nevertheless, the startled dog retreated.

"Eight months: Has walked around her playpen and furniture since before she was 8 mos. Very strong. Can't make her sit down." This short entry my mother made in my baby book gives me a glimpse of my capabilities after eight short months. By this age, I was performing more difficult tasks, which, of course, my brain was directing in an increasingly intelligent way. I was driven to learn how to get about. First, I figured out how to drag myself along the floor. Then, as my body grew stronger, I began to crawl, which allowed me to travel farther and explore more of my environment.

I was very curious about my environment, and the more I could explore, the happier I was. By eight months, I was walking around the playpen and furniture, having learned how to pull myself up onto my feet and how to lean on any convenient support for balance. This extended my reach even further. I could sidestep along the couch and reach for the telephone, turn the knobs on the stereo, and explore whatever I found on the coffee table.

In fact, on this particular day, I find a *pen* on the coffee table. I see it, I reach for it, I grasp it—see how far I've come?—and I put it in my mouth. My ever-vigilant mother quickly swaps it for a teething ring. The pen is now discernible to me and has become an object to suck on. But the pen is in good company, as I will put just about anything I come across in my mouth.

In another entry I read, *"Nine months: She looks very much like [her father]. Big blue eyes—brown hair—light complexion—good natured, although she doesn't smile too easily—keeps a straight face until it's embarrassing when someone is trying to make her smile."*

I can only guess that whoever was trying to make me smile wasn't, in my eyes, funny. This description, "good natured, although she doesn't smile too easily," is *still* an accurate description of my temperament. It's kind of strange to realize that a large part of who I am today is who I already was at nine months old. The entry continues:

> *Kicks her legs when she doesn't want to get in her playpen or highchair . . .*
> *When I take her back up she sighs and makes a contented sound, and puts her fat little arms around my neck.*
> *Also holds a conversation with [her father]. Makes all sorts of grunts and sounds when he talks to her.*
> *When I feed her she waves her arms all around. I have to give her a toy or something to keep her hands busy.*

By nine months I was busily interacting with my parents—desiring, enjoying, and thriving from their attention. I was developing preferences and had no difficulty communicating my likes and dislikes. In this case, I preferred my mother over the highchair.

Our dog, Cindy, could communicate her likes and dislikes, too. She liked being scratched behind the ears and disliked being yelled at. She liked breakfast and disliked the mailman. Cindy and I were not very different at that point in my development. We liked what we liked and didn't like what we didn't like. Life was simple, or, more accurately, *we* were simple—very simple emotional / cognitive creatures.

This early time was a wondrous time. I was on a ship out of my control, for I was not in charge of the biological processes my body was undergoing. Yet I also found myself at the helm of this ship, and I needed to navigate all the uncharted, turbulent waters I encountered during my development. It was an overwhelmingly complex time, and it is certainly understandable if I threw a fit now and then.

The waters became more challenging, the hazards greater, but both captain and ship were becoming ever more capable of negotiating those complex waters. My mental capacities were growing in synchronicity with my body, and my curiosity about the world intensified with my body's increased capacity to motor about and explore it.

When we look at all that a baby accomplishes over her first few months, it seems like an incredible amount of work. But then I think of the seedling and how it reaches inexorably for the sun. That is work, too, but the seedling reaches because this is what it does; it is in its nature, in its very design, to grow toward the sun.

The child is also built to do what she is doing: to grow, to learn about her world, and to master her growing body. The child naturally envelops and embraces these things. In this regard, the process is not work, it is the child's nature. It is in the child's very design.

In *my* design.

And, as the months passed by, all of my energies were devoted precisely to this, and I increasingly learned to interact with my environment like any other warm-blooded intelligent animal. I went after what I liked and avoided what I disliked. My feelings guided my responses. If I felt frightened of something, I kept away from it. If I felt angry with something, I acted aggressively toward it. If I felt pleased with something, I sought it out.

And then, at around eighteen months, something extraordinary began to happen. I began to realize that the face looking back from the mirror was . . . me. Until that time I might have been enthralled with the face in the mirror, but that's all it was—a face in the mirror. Now it had become *my* face.

I tested this idea by watching myself in the full-length mirror at the end of the hallway. I bounced up and down, rocked side to side, and the figure in the mirror bounced and rocked with me. I turned around, and so did she. I reached out to touch the mirror just as her fingertips reached out to touch mine.

These experiments helped build an increasing awareness of myself as something distinct and separate from my environment. It demonstrated that I was not only experiencing my environment, I was beginning to experience "I."

This may not sound like a big achievement, but my dog, Cindy, will never recognize herself in a mirror. Most animals can't, although even as I work on this chapter my cat, Squirrel, has begun hissing at her own reflection. Clearly she sees a cat—ironically, it is one she is telling to *back off.*

There is evidence that some primates recognize themselves in a mirror, however, so at this early point in my development I could perhaps be compared to a chimpanzee. But not for long. For the chimpanzee, self-recognition is its crowning glory. For me, it was just another marker along the road, a marker that appeared quite early in the journey. Where the chimp's developmental path culminates, mine was barely beginning.

7

Human Development

The Intellectual Stage

I look at an early photograph of myself taken when I was about two years old. In it, I am standing and looking off into the distance with my hands behind my back. Next to me sits our dog, Cindy. Her legs are splayed, as if she's just hastily and somewhat reluctantly obeyed the order to sit. Her floppy ears are perked up, and she is looking off in the opposite direction from me. My father, the photographer, had to work fast for that picture, I am sure. Both Cindy and I look ready to wander off, and each seems more interested in something going on outside the camera's frame of reference. We both appear to understand my father's instructions to stay put and are doing what we can to comply, although it is obvious that neither of us understands why we are being required to stay where we are. While we both understand "stay," neither of us understands "photography."

In another photo taken at the same time, I am holding a red carnation in my left hand. I assume that my father placed the carnation there and told me to hold it and to stand in place. In both photos, however, I am looking off to the side and am barely smiling. My father preferred his subjects to look at the camera and smile, so I assume that I couldn't yet follow *all* his instructions, just enough to set up both shots. I also know that my clean, soft skin, the blue corduroy overalls I am dressed in, and my two little pigtails are the product of my mother's love and care. I did not do any of those things myself.

When I look at this little toddler in the photo, so alert and ready to amble off, I marvel at how far she has come since her first moments in the womb as a rapidly dividing bundle of cells. I also marvel at how far she has to go. In a lot of ways, she has barely gotten started. Physically, most of her growing is still ahead of her. Cognitively, she is still learning the layout of the land, and her emotions are unregulated, intense, and guide her actions. Absolutely everything about her is immature.

This two-year-old, it turns out, is telling me something important about phases of development. While it is true that one phase must precede another, a preceding phase does not need to be complete for the next phase to begin. This is a little difficult to understand, because experience tells us that we complete phase one before moving to phase two, read chapter 1 before beginning chapter 2, or pass the introductory class before moving to the intermediate.

However, the process of development works very differently. A phase simply has to reach a particular point of development, and once enough groundwork has been laid, the next stage begins. For a two-year-old, it's like being in both the first and second grades and then, on top of that, beginning the third grade at the same time.

The fact is that although a child's emotional and cognitive development can only begin when an adequate physical framework exists—that is, the body, brain, and nervous system—this phase begins while the physical framework is immature. In fact, cognitive and emotional development commences in earnest shortly after birth.* Now *that's* immature. However, the brain does not physically mature

---

* I assume that every phase of development actually begins long before an observer may see actual signs of it (with the exception of physical development, which we know begins at conception). Consciousness most likely begins in the womb. An observer might be able to point to a moment in development when he or she can recognize consciousness, but this should not be confused with

before it engages in intelligent activities. As mentioned in the last chapter, the brain matures *because* of intelligent activities.

Since conception, I have been undergoing a developmental process that requires an attribute or power be used long before its development is complete. In fact, it is *this very use* that enables an attribute or power to develop.

In the womb, as a tiny embryo, I was a magnificent bundle of biological activity as I proceeded through my prenatal stage of development. My heart began to beat as soon as there were enough cells to support such an action, but long before it could function properly on its own or perform the task it was designed to handle. My digestive system passed amniotic fluid in preparation for the day it would be required to process food. My nervous system and brain developed with the aid of the womb's limited stimulation. When my forming hands brushed against a surface, an impulse traveled along my forming nervous system, and the cells in my forming brain that received the stimulus became responsible for that bit of information from then on.

This developmental law—that I must use an attribute in order to develop and perfect it—governed my development as much after my birth as it did before. The powers of my intelligence—my cognitive and emotional attributes—had to be used and exercised in order to develop. I learned to navigate my world in increasingly purposeful ways with this strengthening power, and it was by using these developing powers that they became strengthened, indeed that they developed at all.

And so we find a two-year-old who is barely on her feet, still learning how to get around in any kind of intelligent way, who is at the mercy of some powerful emotions, and in whose mind a strange new idea—*I am*—is beginning to form.

This is a time in every child's development that has been dubbed by beleaguered parents as the "terrible twos." Parents lament the loss of their cooperative "angel," finding in her place a comparative stranger who resists them, whose favorite declaration seems to be "me do," whose automatic response is "no," and who is prone to violent outbursts.

But here is this enormous idea: *I am.* How does a two-year-old turn this glimmer of self-awareness into full-blown self-consciousness? A good start is by learn-

---

when it *begins*. Research indicates that emotional and cognitive development also begins in the womb (Vaughan, *How Life Begins*, 202). Again, no one can say precisely *when* it begins; researchers only know when it becomes discernible to them. Yet all these things do have a beginning, regardless of how unimpressive and inconspicuous as it may be.

ing what I am *not*. I say "no" to Mom, thus proving *I am not Mom*. I say "no" to Dad and prove *I am not Dad*. I am forming a sense of "I" and learning that *I am not you*.

At the same time, I am learning, *I like this, but I don't like that*. Or, *I want to cuddle when I want to cuddle, and I don't always want to cuddle*. And so I resist snuggling one moment and seek it the next. Partnered with the concept of "I am" is the emerging power of free will, of volition. Around two years of age I am realizing that I am an autonomous operator. I can choose. *I* can choose.

This time in the child's development is extremely important (although parents are often too tired to appreciate it). It is also every bit as exciting for the child as it appears to be. The child is *not* being dramatic. What is *happening* to her is dramatic. It is *huge*. For during this time, the child's rudimentary intellectual powers are making their first appearance.

But what exactly are intellectual powers?

Intellectual powers are powers of the mind. Think about all the things of which your mind is capable. You can imagine one thing (say, a brown furry teddy bear) or many things (say, a roomful of teddy bears of all sizes and colors). You can stick your finger into the image and, in your mind's eye, swirl it around and watch the teddy bears swish apart like so much water. You can line them back up in a neat row and count them. You can categorize them. First by color—all the red ones go here, the yellow ones here. Or line them up by size—from teensy-weensy ones to life-sized ones. Throw one in as tall as the Empire State Building while you're at it. You can take one teddy bear and study its parts: two arms, two legs, stitching for both the nose and toes, black glass eyes, mohair fur, stitched together with upholstery thread, and stuffed with excelsior.

This type of mental exercise may seem simple and pointless, but this same power is used to figure out some very big things. Now try this one.

Imagine you are on a moving train. You drop a stone from the train and—because in this scenario there is no air resistance—watch it fall straight down to the ground. Now imagine you are standing by the tracks, watching the train speed by as the stone drops. From that point of view the stone falls, not in a straight line, but in a parabolic curve. The question is, does the stone actually fall in a straight line or on a parabola?

In this example things begin to get more complicated. It is, in fact, a thought experiment designed by Albert Einstein to introduce the topic of relativity.[1]

Teddy bears and relativity may be light years apart, yet in both cases you are utilizing your intellectual powers.

But what do these exercises show us? They show the types of things our minds can do. The teddy bear exercise, for example, demonstrates that the mind

- is able to form mental images,
- can see things as a whole, such as one complete teddy bear,
- can use symbols, such as the phrase "teddy bear" or its mental image, to represent the actual object,
- has the power of recall, even including fanciful images, such as these imaginary teddy bears, and
- can figure things out, step-by-step, such as how to put a teddy bear together.

Although some important capacities of the intellect are imagination, memory, and the ability to form mental pictures, the intellect also makes extensive use of the power of reason. A simple example of reasoning is, if A=B and B=C, then A=C. From our reasoning we can draw conclusions.

A teddy bear the size of the Empire State Building could not exist in fact. Yet such unrealistic images can lead to actual leaps of insight: Einstein imagined himself riding alongside a beam of light, something that could never happen in reality. Yet this is only one example of the thought experiments he conducted that led him to actual working theories.

Einstein conducted brilliant thought experiments but still needed to prove his theories. Without testing that which seems reasonable, many of the things we believe to be true would never be exposed for the absolute misconceptions that they are.

It was long believed, for example, that flies, worms, and other small animals form spontaneously from rotting material. This idea, called "spontaneous generation," dates back to Aristotle (384–22 B.C.).

It's not difficult to understand why spontaneous generation was accepted as true. Flies, worms, and all kinds of slimy things are often found in and around putrefying matter and apparently come from nowhere. Thus one can reason, "If you leave something to rot, you get flies and mold; therefore, rotting material produces flies and mold." The problem with this line of reasoning, however, is that it simply isn't true. Nevertheless, spontaneous generation remained an unquestioned tenet for more than two thousand years, when the experiments of Louis Pasteur (1822–95) disproved it. Pasteur demonstrated that heating and excluding airborne particles prevent the appearance of flies and other kinds of growth and that microorganisms were innumerable and could travel on air. (In Aristotle's day, no one knew about microorganisms.) Pasteur not only solved the puzzle of where flies and mold actually come from (flies come from flies and mold comes from mold), he also solved the problem of where infections come from during surgery. His discoveries revolutionized our understanding of how disease is spread, as well as of how infection could be minimized during surgery. The number of lives that have been saved as a result of Pasteur's work can only be guessed.

As this story demonstrates, while the powers of imagination and reasoning can certainly construct some believable explanations, these explanations can turn out to be completely wrong. Only through testing what we think is true can we learn the actual truth.

At age two, all of these powers of the intellect belonged to my future. But I was already showing signs that my development was moving right along. By the time I was two, with my mother's assistance, I could take a crayon from the shoebox full of crayons, drag it across a piece of paper, and delight in the waxy blue trail the crayon left behind.

This little maneuver demonstrates that I had developed to the point where I could not only grasp a pen with my hand, I could also grasp it with my mind. I understood that a pen can make marks on a piece of paper. Pens, crayons, and pencils were all the same to me. I liked crayons the best, as they were fat, easy to grip, and colorful. I had been watching my sisters color with them in their books and had learned that there was something to do with crayons besides eat them. My coordination was not yet refined enough to fill the outlined pictures with color the way my sisters did. My strokes were broad and uncontrolled, and it was all I could do to keep the crayon on the paper. At that time, my sisters did not allow me near their coloring books for fear of the carnage I would commit with my crayon.

Over the next year, I developed better control of my crayon and began to draw circles and triangles. And, by the time I was four, I found myself laboriously copying four symbols:

J A N E

Each letter symbolized a sound. I could hear the sound both in my head and when I spoke it aloud.

"Jay . . . Aye . . . En . . . Ee."

Put together, I knew what those sounds and symbols meant, "That spells 'Jane.'"

This was a great intellectual feat, for it demonstrated that I was beginning to think with symbols and understood that one thing could be used to represent another thing. My parents and sisters had taught me how to draw these particular symbols, and I was learning that somehow, when put together, they meant my name—JANE.

It was a puzzle, and one I yearned to solve. I understood that when my father read to me, it was because he knew what all those marks on the page meant. I wanted to read, too, so that I could read stories the way he did. My sisters were reading picture books, decoding them with various amounts of expertise, sounding out words, and deciphering sentences. Kathy was even beginning to venture into big books without pictures. And at Christmastime, I watched them joyfully composing their wish list and decorating it with drawings of snowmen and candy canes. I wanted to be able to write my own list and draw snowmen the way they did.

Reading and writing were just a small sampling of the possibilities and promise I was beginning to discover about my world. I also understood the concept of *photograph* now, and even if I couldn't use a camera myself, I knew how to pose and that I would get to see a picture of myself (my favorite subject) as a result. Life had become a very exciting affair, and the world had become a place of infinite possibilities. In fact, by the age of four, my imagination seemed to have burst its fetters, and I could hardly differentiate between what could and couldn't be, or the difference between reality and fantasy. As far as I was concerned, if I thought of it, it was possible. The force of gravity was unknown to me; therefore, the possibility of flying like Peter Pan was perfectly reasonable, and so were eight reindeer pulling a sleigh through the air with a jolly fat man in it. *Time* was still a vague concept, and so it was reasonable that this same jolly man could deliver presents to every child in the world in one night.

Let's face it, the world is a complete mystery to a four-year-old, and wild fancies determine much of what a child believes. The creaking of a floorboard after dark becomes a monster. The monster has big hands with long fingers and hides under the bed, just waiting to make a grab for the unwary ankle. (And don't ask a four-year-old to *prove* there is a monster under the bed, because everybody knows that when you turn on the light it will just go somewhere else, like the closet, or become invisible, or powerless, but it certainly isn't *gone*.)

Fortunately, as time went by, my imagination would become one component of a larger, more complex intellectual process. It would become the beginning of things, instead of the end-all and be-all. It would help me become interested in things, help me come up with ideas, but would eventually stop being the author of everything I believe.

I had by then realized that the world was full of interesting, inexplicable phenomena. What are clouds, for example, and how do they stay up? Where did all these rocks come from? What is lightning? What is the sky, and how high up is it? As a seven-year-old, I wondered, if a plane flew too high, would it hit the sky? A better-informed playmate told me that when a plane hit the sky, its engine would stall. It sounded reasonable to *me*.

But if I wanted to choose a phenomenon that best symbolizes my journey from awed wonder to (awed) comprehension, it would have to be the rainbow. Both mysterious and beautiful, the rainbow has fascinated me for as long as I can remember. That glowing ephemeral arc of shining color can still make me stop in my tracks and suspend all thought.

As a young child, I could no more explain a rainbow than I could the moon, stars, sun, or sky. A rainbow, like Santa Claus, simply was. What made the rainbow different from other indecipherable mysteries was that I could actually make this object of unparalleled beauty myself. All I needed was the garden hose and some sunshine. Since our garden hose was constantly employed to help us all cool off during the summer, I had the opportunity to make a lot of rainbows. All I needed to do was screw the nozzle onto the hose, and I was in business. I would become totally absorbed as I adjusted the spray from the nozzle and turned this way or that, raising or lowering the hose, watching my rainbow as it dimmed or brightened. I was looking for that delicate and crucial combination that would make the most brilliant and perfect rainbow possible. I wanted to find exactly that moment, that position, that setting, in which the rainbow would flash brightly from the mist, a luminescent arc of vibrant color.

I never did create the perfect rainbow. But, by attempting to do so, I discovered all kinds of things about them. I learned that the rainbow faded as I turned toward the sun and brightened as I turned away. I learned that there is a relationship between the sun, the water, and the rainbow. Rainbows couldn't be created on cloudy days, nor could they be created unless the spray from the hose was very fine. By trying to walk through or under my rainbows without success—they inevitably vanished as I was about to do so—I learned that I was a part of the water-sun-rainbow relationship, as well.

The rainbow escorted me into the intellectual world of science. As I grew older and began studying the sciences in school, I learned that sunlight contains all the colors of the rainbow, all the colors visible to the human eye, and even some wavelengths of light *not* visible. I learned that a rainbow is produced when the sun's light is refracted through mist to form a spectral arc across the sky. I learned that a critical relationship connects the viewer and the sun, as the sun needs to be at one's back and at a certain angle in the sky in order for a rainbow to be seen.

Of course, I learned none of this by playing with the garden hose. Rather, I learned from the experiments of others. I learned about these things only because I was educated by those who already understood such subjects. Captivated as a young child by the beauty of the rainbow, I was motivated to understand it—initially via the garden hose, and then, as my intellectual capacity grew, via the sciences. At the same time, I was learning more than how rainbows are made or the nature of light. I was learning why planes can't actually hit the sky. I was also learning about people, places, cultures, countries, languages, history, and mathematics.

All the while, I was also forming a tighter relationship with the pen. I live in a culture that transmits information with the pen; we are a culture that *writes things down*. At the beginning of every school year I received my textbooks, each one devoted to a particular topic. School would have been a hard proposition indeed if I couldn't read my textbooks. And so, when my formal education began, the skills of reading and writing became a primary focus.

Like every other kind of development, my intellectual development was non-linear, and I was learning all kinds of things simultaneously. Although I needed to know how to read and write to get through school, I didn't learn to read and write before I began learning other things. Everything was interwoven.

Every year the information we were asked to comprehend became a bit more complex and required more analysis. The books we were required to read became a bit more difficult, and the essays we were required to write grew longer. And while I honed my reading and writing skills, these same skills assisted me in learning about other places, other cultures, the nature of the rainbow, and a myriad other things I never knew existed.

Throughout childhood, my intellectual powers increasingly established ascendancy over my emotional and cognitive powers. My emotional and cognitive powers still gave me loads of information that could get me swiftly out of danger. While I was pedaling my bicycle down the road, these powers are what would help me swerve out of the path of the barking dog that had just dashed out at me. When I was three years old, I'd have been content to escape the danger and avoid it in the future. By the time I was riding a bicycle, however, my intellectual powers had developed enough for me to want to come up with a better strategy than simple avoidance.

Unlike the problems a young animal might face, most of my problems did not center around survival. They had nothing to do with finding food, being at-

THE UNIVERSE WITHIN US

tacked, or being eaten. But they were still problems. As my mind matured, for example, I began to notice inconsistencies between what people said and what they did. Sometimes I received conflicting information from two different authority figures. These problems required me to stop, think, and reason my way toward a solution. At age three, I didn't know that these kinds of problems existed. But by the time I was six, I had definitely become aware of them.

When I was in the first grade, like all good Catholic children at that time, I was being prepared for my first confession and first communion. During one particular lesson, my teacher, Sister Carmeline, told us quite firmly that if we took holy communion or went to confession less than once a month, we would go to hell. Period.

Her words shook me to the core. I had never seen my parents go to confession *or* take holy communion. According to Sister Carmeline, this meant they were going to hell! Here I was being presented with two conflicting pieces of information from my most important authority figures—my teacher and my parents. How could I make sense of this? My mind raced, and I quickly reasoned my way to a conclusion. It was simple and went like this: "Mom and Dad don't go to confession or communion. Mom and Dad are *not* going to hell. Therefore Sister Carmeline is *wrong*." Maybe I didn't use quite that language. But I certainly came to that conclusion. Poor Sister Carmeline's credibility took a big fall that day.

Of course, it would be many more years before I was ready to tangle with the Catholic concepts of hell and sacraments. And the path of my reasoning was much simpler then. It followed this logic: "Mom and Dad are right; therefore, if you disagree with them, you're wrong." At six years old, I knew unequivocally that Mom and Dad were never wrong.

My absolute certainty about my parents' infallibility was about to come to a swift demise, however. It ended abruptly the day I punched the girl next door (who was my age) for telling me that there was no Santa Claus.

I *knew* Santa Claus was real. He showed up every Christmas Eve in the flesh, didn't he? Mom and Dad opened the door to him and let us take his cold North Pole oranges, didn't they? I heard him talking to children on the radio, ho-ho-hoing, and asking them what they wanted for Christmas, didn't I?

The fact is, I *loved* Santa Claus. He loved children so much that he brought us toys every year. It made Christmas my favorite time of year. At my neighbor's declaration of Santa's nonexistence, I became outraged, and in an angry burst of self-righteous indignation, I punched her and ran home to tell Mom about the horrible thing Paula had said.

But Mom didn't respond the way I thought she would. She was far from outraged. In fact, she reluctantly admitted to me that there was no Santa Claus.

Trembling, I tried to choke back my tears. No Santa Claus! My mom was telling me there was no Santa Claus! Shaken, embarrassed, disappointed, I could barely form my next question, "What about the Easter Bunny?"

She shook her head.

No Easter Bunny!

"The tooth fairy?"

Imagine my relief when she said, "YES, there is a tooth fairy!"

It was a humiliating moment when I had to call Paula and tell her that she was right, that there was no Santa Claus, and apologize for hitting her. But after the shock wore off and I was able to calm down, I was left with the most disconcerting realization of all—my parents had *lied* to me about Santa Claus and the Easter Bunny. What else might they have lied about?

Through direct lies, or by simply being mistaken, adults were quickly becoming unreliable sources of information.

These incidents, as disturbing as they were at the time, forced me to engage my intellectual powers, forced me to think, reason, and analyze. While upsets like these may have been a source of outrage or tears initially, they also assisted my intellectual development. And the fact that these incongruities had become visible to me was evidence of my increasing intellectual capacity.

At the same time that I was learning my ABCs, I was being introduced to some concepts that the Catholic faith is built upon. These abstract concepts included topics such as sin, heaven, hell, and the sacraments. At six years old, as I was being prepared for first confession and first communion, my understanding of these concepts was quite simple and, as I was incapable of thinking in abstracts, quite literal and physical.

Heaven, on the one hand, was up in the sky and was where good people went when they died. Lots of people wearing white robes were gathered there, and tranquil harp music played in the background. Everyone was well, happy, and content. Hell, on the other hand, was down in the earth. Everything was on fire there. In fact, fire was the only source of light. Everyone was sick and miserable. It was where bad people went when they died. You went to hell if you committed a mortal sin.

Purgatory was a temporary place of residence for the vast majority of people, a place of temporary punishment, like a prison term, at the end of which you would be released and go to heaven. I imagined purgatory to be like a windowless waiting room or train station, with hard benches to sit upon. Not the best of places to be, but not the worst, either.

Sin, I believed, was breaking the rules of the Church, and the sacraments acted as an antidote to sin. The sacrament of baptism was performed within weeks of birth in order to rid the child of original sin and to keep it from going to limbo if he or she died. Limbo was the place unbaptized babies went because you could only go to heaven if you had been baptized. Since babies are sinless, they couldn't go to hell or purgatory. And so there was limbo. (This particular concept is no longer taught by the Catholic Church.) I imagined limbo as a vast, airy ocean teeming with babies.

The sacrament of confession helped keep our souls clean by regular confession of sins to a priest, who serves as God's intermediary. After hearing the confession, the priest then assigns performance of a penance, which usually consists of a number of prayers. Another sacrament, called extreme unction, is performed shortly before death and is also necessary to make entry into heaven possible.

By six years old, I knew for certain that I was a sinner. Sin, as I understood it, was anything a child did that could be called naughty. It was a sin to fight. It was a sin to be disobedient to my mother or father. It was a sin to lie. Good behavior made grownups happy. Sinful—or bad—behavior made them angry. When I was being good, I wasn't sinning. When I was bad, I was. It was that simple.

When I had to go to confession, I could easily come up with a list of sins—I hit my brother once, I disobeyed my mother twice, I lied twice. I rarely reported sins I remembered committing. Instead, I authored a list of likely infractions. I made efforts to keep it reasonable, and now and then I would throw in something unusual, like confessing that I had used a swear word.

At six, seven, and eight years of age, I never wondered why I confessed the things I did; in fact, *fabricating* my list of sins would have been a more accurate term. I mean, a child does not keep an actual list of sins. She just assumes she has broken the rules and has to come up with a list because she is going to confession and has to confess something.

I didn't wonder why lying was a sin for me but wasn't a sin for my parents, such as their lying to me about Santa Claus. I lived, after all, in a world where there were different rules for adults and children. My parents got to stay up later than I did to watch TV. They drank coffee in the morning, while I drank milk. They drove the car, something only adults were allowed to do. My father went to work, and I went to school. It wasn't a question of right or wrong for all, it was just that it was wrong for kids to do some things (like drink coffee or tell a lie) that were

OK for adults to do. In fact, as stunned as I was that Mom and Dad had lied to me about Santa Claus, I had no problem helping them perpetrate the lie for my younger brother and sisters. It made me feel grown up to know something the younger kids didn't.

By the time I was nine years old, however, the idea that being good came by way of obeying the rules was beginning to unravel. I was becoming aware of a new kind of incongruity, one that made me very uncomfortable. I was beginning to notice problems that the rules couldn't solve. Sometimes it seemed that it was by following the rules that things actually went wrong.

A story, for example, told by my fourth-grade teacher, Sister Albertus, was intended to convey a lesson about sacrifice and humility. It went something like this: "A poor old woman with only two pennies to her name went to Sunday mass. She sat way in the back of the church. Lots of rich children came in and sat in the front. When the collection basket was passed, the children showed off by tossing their coins noisily into the basket. But when the basket reached the old lady, she put her last two pennies in *very quietly*."

This story troubled me deeply. I understood what it meant to convey, but the intended moral was eclipsed by a nagging thought: "Why would the church take the last two pennies from a poor old lady?"

I couldn't solve this dilemma. There was an aspect to this story that couldn't be solved by what I was learning in catechism. I didn't even consider asking Sister Albertus. She had told the story in order to tell us two things: be humble and sacrifice. This story, like so many others, did not require discussion. But my mind went over and over it.

Why would the church take the last two pennies from a poor old lady?

I could just picture her. She lived alone with her scraggly cat in a little one-room shack. Her long gray skirt was worn and ragged, and her gloves had holes in the fingers. One lump of coal in the stove was all she had to keep her warm. She had probably given her kitty the last of the milk before she put on her kerchief, tied it under her chin, and hobbled out the front door. She hobbled not because she was old but because she was weak from hunger. Finally, she made it to the church and was glad to sit down and have a rest for a while.

And then the mass began. She stood, and knelt, and sat, and prayed, and listened to the sermon. Then the collection basket, row by row, made its way toward the back. It reached her and paused in front of her. She stretched out her hand, her last two pennies nestled in her palm, and . . . here I would freeze the image.

It's just *wrong*, was all I could think, for the church to take her last two pennies. But why was I thinking that?

I knew the rules of the church. I knew that the church expected us to sacrifice. I knew that we were supposed to put money in the collection basket. So why was I disregarding the point of the story? Why was I instead focusing on the other issue that I didn't dare ask about?

This was just a story my teacher told us one day about a fictional old lady and a collection basket. I heard not only her story but another story—one that didn't put the Church in a very good light. I heard it because I had become capable of hearing it. I heard it because I was entering yet another phase of my development.

During this phase, I would begin to hear things I hadn't heard before and see things I hadn't seen before. In fact, this new phase of development would eventually add new dimensions to just about every situation I would find myself in.

8

Human Development

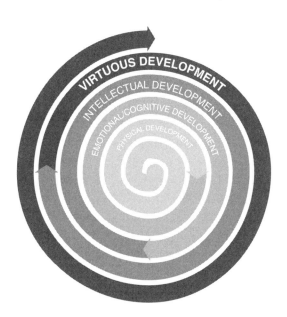

The Virtuous Stage

I am three or four years old and on my little red tricycle. I am trying my best to run over a big, fat, red ant. I can't seem to do it. I pedal forward and back. There it is, unflattened. I try again, forward three pedals, and back three pedals. The ant trundles along unscathed, oblivious to the rolling destruction towering above it.

Intent upon my mission of destruction, I pedal forward and back, forward and back, forward and back.

It is a strange memory, isolated and meaningless. Nevertheless, I have always remembered the incident. Perhaps I remember it only as a puzzling and frustrating moment. It should have been easy to squash that ant. It turned out to be impossible.

But now I look at this incident as an important indicator of a time in my life before compassion, a time in which I was not feeling or displaying empathy. Yet I am capable of both compassion and empathy now. These days, I rap on my kitchen counter if I find little sugar ants scouting about and give them time to retreat before I begin using the space. Or if they become too numerous, I spread pennyroyal oil around their most traveled paths since they are repelled by its minty aroma. I know it's "just an ant," but if I squish it, there is something in *me* that feels that squish, too. I seem to experience a little death myself, and it's an unpleasant sensation. And so, I seek alternate solutions. I seem to win only if we all win.

I look at both behaviors as two points along a continuum. What is it that causes these two behaviors to be so different? At the early end of the continuum, I am intent on crushing the ant in a methodical, deliberate way. At the other end, I sympathize with the ant and try to figure out how to make things work for us both.

The answer lies in my response to the story of the old lady and the collection basket. This was a glimmer of a new developmental dimension that would eventually have me rapping on my kitchen counter to scare off ants. For what I was trying to solve at the tender age of nine was an *ethical* dilemma. I knew the church didn't need those two pennies the old lady dropped in the collection basket, while her life probably depended on them. Was it right or wrong for the Church to expect her to give something she needed so badly, something the Church didn't need at all? If she gave her last two pennies, she might not be able to buy food. She might starve to death. Was she wrong to give the last of her money? Would she be wrong to keep it? Would keeping the money mean she wasn't following the Church's teachings about being humble and sacrificial? But, by wanting her last two pennies, didn't that make the Church greedy and selfish? So went my thinking, round and round, loop after loop.

I was wrestling with the questions of "right action" and "wrong action," a right and wrong the rules I had been learning didn't address, a right and wrong that went beyond the expectations of my superiors. The drive to wrestle with this dilemma was a sign that the virtuous phase of my development had begun.

But what, exactly, are virtuous powers? Consider Christ's parable of the Good Samaritan, with which so many of us are familiar:

A certain man went down from Jerusalem to Jericho, and fell among thieves, which stripped him of his raiment, and wounded him, and departed, leaving him half dead. And by chance there came down a certain priest that way: and when he saw him, he passed by on the other side. And likewise a Levite, when he was at the place, came and looked on him, and passed by on the other side. But a certain Samaritan, as he journeyed, came where he was: and when he saw him, he had compassion on him. And went to him, and bound up his wounds, pouring in oil and wine, and set him on his own beast, and brought him to an inn, and took care of him. And on the morrow, when he departed, he took out two pence, and gave them to the host, and said unto him, Take care of him; and whatever thou spendest more, when I come again, I will repay thee.[1]

The hero of the story, the Samaritan, demonstrates how virtuous powers are manifested—through right action. When the Samaritan came upon the scene he felt *compassion*. When one feels compassion, one is sharing the suffering of another. To feel, to share, to experience something someone else is experiencing— what an extraordinary power! The Samaritan is *motivated* by compassion, not by thought of a reward (the victim has been stripped, and the Samaritan doesn't know if he is rich or poor), and not because he hopes to impress anyone (there is no one to witness his actions). His virtuous powers give him the capacity to feel compassion, and he quickly translates that feeling into right action.

This parable helps us examine virtuous behavior (right action), as well as the alternatives (wrong action). In fact, we find three kinds of conduct. The first, as displayed by the thieves, could be called "might makes right." This is the credo of bullies, people devoid of compassion, who feel entitled to take advantage of, or overpower, others for pleasure or gain. The thieves not only felt entitled to rob the traveler, they felt entitled to wound him, strip him, and leave him half dead. This is the lowest form of human conduct.

The second sort of behavior is not so obviously wrong, because while the priest and Levite hadn't hurt the man, they didn't help him either. Perhaps each was afraid that the thieves were not far off and that they might become the next victims. The fact that they each passed by on the other side, however, suggests that they were both repulsed by what they saw and wanted to put some distance between themselves and the man. Perhaps this kind of behavior can be called "self-preservation is right."

But they could also claim that they acted out of obedience to the law. As servants of the Temple, the holiest place in the Jewish world, they were required to abide by certain purity laws, one of which forbade touching a corpse. How could the priest or the Levite know that the man wasn't dead without risking violation of the purity law? This behavior could be called "obedience to the law is right." This can be true.

Certainly, laws and rules exist for good reason. They allow a society to conduct its affairs with a reasonable amount of order. But laws and rules cannot cover every situation, and rigid adherence to them is ultimately a surrender of personal responsibility. When I am driving on my legally assigned side of the road, I will cross into the other lane in order to avoid a collision. Although I would be technically breaking the law, I would certainly be found at fault had I not done everything in my power to avoid an accident.

The Samaritan's response, we are told, was motivated by compassion. By stating clearly that he felt compassion, Christ eliminates speculation about the Samaritan's motives. (We are left to speculate about what motivates the thieves, the priest, and the Levite, most likely because we are all too familiar with these kinds of behaviors.)

It is the Samaritan's compassion that distinguishes him from the other characters in the story. Moreover, the compassion he felt was for a total stranger. This is an important distinction, for who among us does not feel compassion toward those we love? The Samaritan, however, knows nothing about the man lying on the roadside. He may be a thief himself, a murderer even. He may be an enemy of the Samaritan people. Perhaps he had even done something to provoke the attack. But none of these thoughts motivates the Samaritan. All the Samaritan needs to know is that before him is a man badly beaten, stripped, and half dead. He is moved to act.

And what of his action? He could have revived the man, put a blanket around him, helped him into the shade, left him with food and water, and gone on his way. He could have gone ahead and sent back help. Instead the Samaritan did everything within his power to succor the man. In fact, this required some personal sacrifices. He sacrificed his oil and wine—it's doubtful he had packed it for first-aid purposes. He sacrificed his time—who knows what deadlines he missed as a result of this detour? He sacrificed his comfort—by placing the stranger on his own donkey, he now had to proceed on foot. He sacrificed his money—he had no expectations that he would be paid back. In fact, he told the innkeeper he would pay *more*, if necessary. Perhaps we can call the third kind of behavior "treating others as you would have them treat you is right."

What the thieves, the priest, and the Levite have in common is that they all put themselves first. Although the thieves acted in a heinous way, while the priest and Levite did not act at all, both types of actions are motivated by self-interest. The thieves wanted what belonged to the traveler. The priest and Levite feared for their own safety, were repulsed by the sight, didn't want to be inconvenienced, or wanted to preserve their condition of ritual purity. The Samaritan, however, put the interests of the beaten man before his own interests. We know this by the sacrifices he made and by his actions. Through this example, we begin to understand what virtuous behavior looks like and what creates right action.

At two years of age, I began to become aware of "I"—myself as an entity separate and distinct from my environment. Everything else—people, animals, toys, food, candy—was "not me." They were all outside of "I." That's how I knew for sure they weren't me. I learned very quickly the priority of "I" and that the needs of "I" were most important. Everything else either supported or threatened "I," for it could bring pleasure or pain, reward or punishment. The thieves, priest, and Levite all behaved as if "I" had first priority.

As my virtuous powers developed, I began to be nudged away from the idea of the all-importance of "I." Instead I began to care about what happened to others. Of course, this expanding zone of care first enveloped my family and friends. Those are the people I love. When they suffered, I suffered. When something good happened to them, I felt their joy.

My virtuous powers, however, made it possible to expand that zone of concern even further. In fact, this is a central point of this parable:

> And behold a certain lawyer stood up and tempted him, saying Master, what shall I do to inherit eternal life?
>
> He said unto him, what is written in the law? how readest thou?
>
> And he answering said, Thou shalt love the Lord thy God with all thy heart, and with all thy soul, and with all thy strength, and with all thy mind; and thy neighbor as thyself.
>
> And he said unto him, Thou hast answered right: this do and thou shalt live.
>
> But he, willing to justify himself, said unto Jesus, And who is my neighbor?[2]

In response, Jesus spoke the parable of the Good Samaritan, then asked the lawyer to answer his own question: "Which now of these three, thinkest thou, was the better neighbor unto him that fell among the thieves?"[3]

The lawyer answered, "He that shewed mercy on him."[4]

Christ's response to the lawyer was simple: "Go and do likewise."[5]

The point is this: you have the capacity to turn each person you encounter into your neighbor. Loving your neighbor as yourself has nothing to do with who the other person is. We each have the capacity to turn that other person into our neighbor; we each have the capacity to love that other person as ourselves. Our virtuous powers give us this capacity.

By age nine, I was beginning to experience the awareness of other people as my neighbors as Christ describes it. When someone becomes my neighbor, it means the welfare of that person is becoming as important to me as my own welfare. When I became concerned about the welfare of the old lady, she had moved from simply "other" and had become my neighbor. A stranger to me, perhaps, yet a stranger I felt compassion for.

The intellectual capacity allows us to solve all kinds of problems. Virtuous powers give us the ability to solve problems on another's behalf.

When I operate in the world as if my own concerns are the only important ones that matter, I act like the priest and the Levite. To tell the truth, I recognize myself in the actions of the priest and Levite. I often choose the path of non-involvement, either out of fear or because I do not want to make the required sacrifices. Yet this is not a behavior I am satisfied with. When I act as if the other person's concerns are as important as my own, I act more like the Samaritan. But the Samaritan actually didn't act merely as if another's welfare was as important as his own. Instead, he behaved as if the concerns of the injured man were *more* important than his own. We know this because of one thing, his actions. His right action.

The thieves acted both wrongly and illegally. The priest and the Levite did nothing legally wrong; nevertheless, they acted wrongly. The Samaritan, behaving in a virtuous way by putting the welfare of another before his own, acted rightly. The Samaritan, in fact, displayed the highest of human qualities possible, and he achieved full human stature by his actions. Simply put, you just can't get more human than when you are acting virtuously. And it is here that we find ourselves face-to-face with the definition of a human being. For only when a person acts with virtue is his human potential finally made manifest.

As it turns out, there are many layers to the parable of the Good Samaritan. Christ chose the Samaritan as the hero in order to make a particular point to his contemporaries. Samaritans accepted both the prophethood of Moses and the five books of the Torah—which are attributed to Moses—but otherwise held divergent beliefs from mainstream Judaism.

The Jews at that time regarded Samaritans with contempt and considered them heretics. By contrast, the priest and the Levite mentioned in the parable belonged to an inherited and elite class of Jewish society. The priests oversaw the animal sacrifices at the Temple in Jerusalem, and the Levites assisted them. Christ's listeners considered priests and Levites their superiors, who were looked up to, while the Samaritans were considered their inferiors and were looked down upon.

Through this parable we hear a simple yet difficult message: class, power, privilege, family lineage, ritual purity—all those things a culture values and promotes—have absolutely no bearing on the true nature of an individual. Birth does not determine the nature or character of a person, nor does status. What makes a person great are two things—his motivation and his resulting action.

And there is yet another message: status, birth, culture, and even the law cannot determine right action. Right action is something apart from—something that transcends—all these things.

As I entered the virtuous phase of my development, this newly emerging power began to affect my thinking and my reasoning. When I thought about what was the right or wrong thing to do, I found myself considering things beyond the expectations of my parents, or a prescribed set of rules, or the most logical solution. I began looking for an action in which everybody won (which should not be confused with "made everybody happy"). This is why the story of the old lady and her last two pennies disturbed me so. Clearly, somebody lost, and it looked like it was the old lady.

As I grew up, I found myself tangling more and more with dilemmas that involved ethical dimensions:

- The time a playmate offered me a quarter. We could go to the neighborhood store, she proposed, buy some candy, and go eat it by the river. The dilemma: my mother had forbidden me to go near the river for fear of my drowning. Would I forfeit my mother's right to trust me for some candy?
- The dilemma of what to do about my younger sister, Anne, six years my junior, who wanted to tag along with me everywhere. A real nuisance!
- The dilemma of whether to confess to my parents that it was *I* who locked my little sister, Mary, inside the bathroom, and not my brother, Mark, who was being blamed at the time.
- Wanting a wooden beverage case from a nearby soda machine as a display unit for my knick-knacks. People took (stole?) milk and beverage cases all the time. The question: is it wrong to do something if everyone else is doing it?

Scenarios like these helped me to develop virtuously in the same way that the rainbow helped me to develop intellectually. Each problem I wrestled with contributed to my virtuous development. Each problem forced me to consider the welfare or proper treatment of others. I knew when I had failed to act with virtue because my conscience was becoming an integral part of my internal workings. When I did something wrong, I felt an odd kind of pain that was almost physical in nature. This pain haunted me as a nagging, subtle feeling of remorse. It was an unpleasant feeling that bogged me down. When I acted with virtue, I felt lighter somehow.

I have included a list of some virtues in Appendix 2 for your perusal. This is certainly a list of high ideals that often feel out of my reach. But just the attempt to meet these ideals makes me a better person. It also makes things harder. Eating candy down by the river was a tempting proposition. It was that component of deserving Mom's trust that snarled things up for me. When ethics and virtues entered a situation, it slowed me down and gave me more to think about. I could no longer think only of myself or only of what I wanted. I had to think about others, too.

Virtuous development is really the push out of the nest of self-centeredness. The more my virtues developed, the less I saw myself as the center of the universe. The less I saw myself as the center of the universe, the less I considered my interests more important than my neighbors', and the more thoughtful I became about what I did. It sure has complicated things.

Virtuous development facilitates personal integration. When acting virtuously, all of our powers are called into action—physical, emotional, cognitive, and intellectual. The Samaritan, I can assume from experience, felt alarmed and outraged when he came upon the beaten and unconscious man. His anger and the burst of adrenaline that was released supplied him with the energy he needed to respond to this emergency. His intellect came up with the solution of cleaning the man's wounds, placing him on his donkey, and bringing him to the inn. His intellect allowed him to think ahead and plan for the possibility that more money might be needed for the man's care. He physically had to help the man onto the donkey and had to walk the donkey to the inn. Had he been too small to lift the man onto the donkey, I am sure he would have had the wits to find assistance.

As my virtuous powers developed, my physical, emotional, and intellectual powers became redirected and began to work together. It is as if my virtuous powers were taming the unruly drives and impulses of my body, emotions, and mind which, left to their own devices, tend to drag me in all directions. Thanks to virtuous development, these aspects of me have begun to work as a team. I absolutely need every power at my disposal, but when virtue directs my actions, what I do with my other powers changes.

In fact, I now find that my virtuous powers give me the capacity to produce a new kind of diagram, one that reflects a divine kind of light.

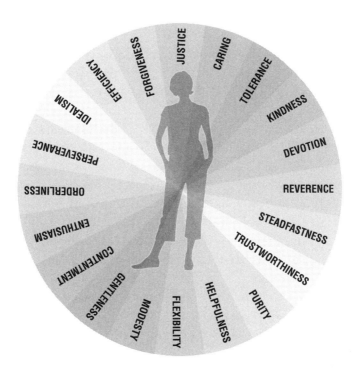

This phase of my development seems to be driving my life now. Day after day I am faced with one ethical challenge after the other as I deal with everything from the rude motorist to the cashier that has short-changed himself. With some challenges I think I do well, while with other challenges I think I do poorly.

All in all I never seem to become proficient at responding with virtue. It is like pushing a boulder up a mountain. It seems as if there are relentless forces working against me that, if I give up or get lazy, will push me back down the slope.

One thing is for certain: the harder the challenge, the more I learn. The tougher the struggle, the greater the gain. I may as well be reconciled to these daily challenges, because this is how it's going to be for the rest of my life.

And I find it is here that I am back in the present, back at that moment of pen-poised-above-paper first mentioned so many pages ago. I realize now that this current phase of development is changing what I write about, and when I pick up my pen, I feel a new kind of responsibility. Certain questions demand an answer. Shall I use the pen to create ill will, or to manipulate the reader with propaganda? Shall I use the pen to clarify a point, or to confuse the reader? Shall I use the pen to titillate, to stir up passions, to guide the malleable toward acts of violence? Or shall I use the pen to stir up souls and inspire acts of great good? What exactly, my virtuous nature demands of me, is my responsibility? The answer to that I am constantly defining.

And will continue to define. I will never arrive at a final answer for the simple reason that my virtuous powers will never reach their potential. Virtuous development, as it turns out, is the developmental phase that will last the rest of my life.

In fact, a characteristic particular to this phase of development is that its potential can *not* be realized in this lifetime. I have certainly reached my peak physically during the time of sexual maturation. In fact, it is part of my natural life cycle that my physical powers will decline as I get older. I have certainly reached my emotional and cognitive peak; intelligence is more or less what it is and does not continue to increase throughout my lifetime. The intellect had also achieved its potential by the time I reached adulthood. I can always work with what I have to gain more knowledge, but the basic tools I have to work with have not themselves increased.

But virtues are, in large part, a mystery to me. I know things work better when I use my virtues. I know I *feel* better, but I don't know why. And it often seems easier *not* to use them. In fact, in the heat of the moment, I often act without them and only think of how they could have been applied much later. They just don't seem to be natural. Virtuously speaking, I feel like a toddler—I'm wobbly and fall a lot.

There's a reason for this, a very *good* reason for these wobbly virtuous legs. It is because I'm still in the early phase of my virtuous development. Virtuous action comes as easily to me as walking did when I was a toddler or as writing did when I was learning how to spell my name. Not easily at all. That's not a problem, however. It's not supposed to be simple. I mean, why should virtuous action come easily, when I've had to learn how to do everything else one step at a time?

Fortunately, we are not left to our own devices. As you will see in the next chapter, this world provides everything we need and is the perfect place to engage in the process of virtuous development.

9

A Perfect World

"Dost thou reckon thyself only a puny form / When within thee the universe is folded?"

This is not a question asking you to examine your girth. After all, one cannot physically encompass the universe. Instead, it is a question that refers to your capacity and powers.

The process that leads to enfolding the universe begins at conception. At the time of birth, you encompassed both the mineral and vegetable kingdoms. That is, you had acquired the powers of attraction and augmentation. After a few years, as your intellect blossomed, you began to encompass and enfold the animal kingdom. As an adult, you manifest the powers of attraction, augmentation, emotion, cognition, and the intellect. You are currently in the virtuous stage of development and have the opportunity to learn how to correctly direct these powers in order to take right action. This is the highest sphere possible in human development, and by reaching it, you do indeed enfold the known universe.

This is a very different perspective from how we generally define a human being or look at the course of our lives. We tend to look at life as if it were a sequence of events—some random, some inevitable—such as graduation from high school, a surgery, a summer vacation, the death of a loved one, a wedding, or an international trip. We often measure and describe our lives by our experiences or the goals we've achieved. Now, however, we can begin to understand that life is not merely a sequence of events but a process during which our human potential develops.

This world is the perfect place for that development to happen. "Perfect" may seem a strange choice of words to describe the world. After all, this is actually an *imperfect* world full of inescapable tests, trials, and suffering. But there is a critical interrelationship between the process of development and the events, mishaps, and problems that occur along the way. Simply put, the tests and trials of the world act as catalysts and further the developmental process. Therefore, it is the world's imperfections that make it so absolutely perfect. Keep this in mind as we take a deeper look into how this world assists all phases of development—phases that culminate in the budding of our virtuous powers.

This world provides a greater environment with which to interact.

We have already seen how the brain is able to develop due to the endless stimulation this world provides. We are more than just a brain, however. We each have a body, which the brain directs. We soon learn that the world is full of things—food, affection, play, shade, sun, rain, spiders—and learn what actions to take in order to acquire the things we like or avoid the things we don't like.

We also begin to learn cause and effect. That is, we do something, and we get a result. The first thing an infant learns is that if he cries when he's hungry, food appears. To an infant, it must seem as if crying produces the food. He also learns that if he cries when his diaper is wet, it is replaced with a dry one. The infant also learns that the world affects him. As far as he knows, hunger and a wet diaper are things that happen to him. But there is something he can do about it—*cry*.

As the child grows and his explorations expand, these continual interactions assist the development of intelligence. He begins to learn the names of things and makes associations. The sun feels warm. Snow is cold. Mosquitoes can sting. This is a television, and pictures appear on it. This is a teddy bear, and I like to take it everywhere with me. This is a bowl filled with cereal, and if I push it off the table I can watch it fall to the floor.

In time the child grows up to become a force that impacts and affects his environment, even as his environment impacts him. Survival demands this of all of us. We need to ensure that we have enough food for the winter. We need to be able to cross a river without drowning. But we want to do more than just survive. We want to understand the world around us. We want to understand what causes lightning. We want to know where illness comes from. The intellect must continuously work to solve these problems and riddles.

Of course, the culmination of this development is the emergence of our virtuous capacity. As we interact with this environment, we must choose how to behave toward our fellow creatures—plants, animals, and other people. Indeed, the most challenging virtuous conundrums are provided by people. We are yelled at unjustly, treated unfairly, have our hopes disappointed, and must constantly choose how to respond to these situations. I sometimes wonder if this is why

Christ tells us to love our enemies, for they provide the greatest challenges, and therefore the greatest opportunities, to further our virtuous development.

We witness, are subject to, and display virtuous and non-virtuous behavior on a daily basis, and it is through our daily ethical interactions that we are able to develop this most advanced aspect of ourselves.

This world offers contrasts and degrees.

A friend of mine recently said to me, "In music and in life, the spaces are just as important as the notes." In other words, in order to have music, we must also have silence. We must have silence before and after the piece, and intervals of silence within the piece itself. If sound were constant, with no silences or spaces, it would be impossible to distinguish any music at all.

In order to be called *music*, the notes must move up and down the scale. One constant note is merely a tone. Notes also differ in duration—some notes are drawn out, others rat-a-tat swiftly. Notes can combine to create harmonious chords. They can also clash with each other and make a jarring noise. In addition, one tune must be different from another. If every piece of music were identical, it would just be a repetition of sound.

In this world of objects, the spaces between them are as important as the objects themselves and allow us to distinguish one object from another. Just as in music, the differences between objects are also important. By appearing in unending variation, objects create a world that is richly textured and endlessly complex.

These objects become known to us through their qualities—their characteristics and properties. We know a stone by its texture, hardness, and weight. We know fire by its heat and light. We know thunder by its sound. We know a rose by its colorful petals and sweet scent. But we also come to know these things by comparing them to each other. The softness of the rose petal contrasts with the hardness of the stone. The heat of fire contrasts with the coldness of ice. The loudness of thunder contrasts with the sigh of a breeze in the grass.

While we learn about objects through their qualities, we also learn about qualities—such as hardness, heat, sound, or light—through objects. We learn that qualities appear in degrees. There are many degrees, for example, between the soft rose petal and the hard stone. There are many degrees between the heat radiating from a cooling cup of tea and the heat from a blazing noon sun. Light can be a faint glimmer, or it can gradually increase to become so bright we need to shield our eyes.

At the intellectual level, knowledge, too, appears in degrees. At the low end of the scale is ignorance—the absence of knowledge. Little by little, as we continuously learn, our knowledge grows. If we could turn knowledge into music, we can imagine that a learned person would need a whole orchestra to play his layered and rich personal tune. By contrast, an ignorant person's tune would consist of long silences punctuated by a few single notes.

Likewise, we witness virtues in varying degrees whenever we see them acted out. We learn about kindness as a child when our mother nurses us through the flu. We learn about compassion when we see someone tend to an injured bird. We also get to see what the absence of virtue looks like. Someone shoots a squirrel for pleasure—certainly this is the absence of compassion. I would call it cruelty. We find ourselves picked on by the school bully—certainly this is the absence of love. I would call it meanness. To simply be uncaring is less obviously cruel, but it is definitely a failure to act virtuously.

In this world we get to experience every degree of virtue as we move up the sliding scale of virtuous possibility. We can witness the disharmonious noise of a person acting without virtue. We can witness the silence of someone not acting at all. And we can witness the inspiring melody of someone acting with virtue. Of course, the only person we get to constantly observe is our self. All these contrasts and degrees of expression give us the opportunity to get to know and truly understand our virtuous powers.

This world gives us a place to practice and to make continuous effort.

Many years ago, there was a hill I liked to head for during walks with my dog, Sybil. It was a grassy bit of slope with a stream at the bottom, and it was bordered by a brambly hedge. It was a good place for me to lie back to watch the clouds drift across the sky and enjoy the peacefulness of my surroundings. Sybil, however, would become alert.

Often, after a few minutes, a rabbit would silently materialize in front of the hedge, soon to be followed by others. Sybil would stand up, watch attentively for a few minutes, take a step forward, and freeze. After another few minutes she would s-l-o-w-l-y take another step forward, then freeze. Ears perked up, eyes wide and focused, every muscle taut, she would make her glacial way down the hill toward her cottontail prey.

"Is today the day?" I would wonder, as I watched Sybil alternately freeze and step forward. "Is today the day she catches a rabbit?"

Finally, with only a few yards remaining, she would spring, tail flashing like a flag behind her—forty-two pounds of determined dog. But the rascally rabbits would have vanished. More relaxed now, with her tail happily wagging, Sybil would trot back and forth along the hedge, nose to the ground, sniffing eagerly—the scent of rabbits the only reward for her patient efforts.

Any time we sat on that hill around dusk, the rabbits came out. Every time Sybil would patiently and excitedly inch her way down the hill. Every time I would believe that this time she'd catch a rabbit.

Only she never did—at least, not that I ever knew. (Who knows what she did when she was off on her own?) It never bothered her, though. For her, every day was a new day that could bring new rabbits. Every day offered a fresh opportunity. For her, the joy was in the effort.

From Sybil I learned that the idea of failure—and its natural offspring, giving up—were a strictly human concoction. I learned that every day—indeed every moment—offers a fresh opportunity. I learned that joy could be found by focusing on effort and practice instead of outcomes.

Babies and children know the joy of effort. A baby laughs as it toddles across the floor with wild careening steps. A young child happily scribbles with a crayon across the page and is proud of the crude triangles and squares she is learning to draw. Children have not yet learned to judge their work; thus, for them, the joy is in the doing, in the practice, and in the effort.

The joy is in the effort on the intellectual level as well. My dad used to say, "If you don't have a wolf at the door, hire one." He knew that life without problems and challenges is more than just dull—it stagnates. We thrive on solving problems and puzzles. Fortunately, there are usually "wolves" at the door of one sort or another. Problems occur daily that need to be dealt with—everything from solving a problem at work to how to live within a budget. Once we solve one problem, we tend to move on to the next. We don't like to rest for long.

Constant effort is particularly crucial to virtuous development, and we certainly have new opportunities for practice every day. To develop virtuously, one must be wide awake, conscious at every moment—thinking, analyzing, and reviewing from moment to moment, and all that inner effort must then be expressed in action.

Remember the actions of the good Samaritan and the avoidance of action by the priest and the Levite? The Samaritan was the one who *showed* mercy. He was the one who made the effort. But no one just wakes up one day a virtuous person. We can only get there by practicing daily and by making the effort. We all start out just as unskilled at compassion as we once were at walking. But there's no better place to practice putting our virtues into action than this physical world.

This world provides teachers.

We are not cast into the world like a shipwrecked sailor on an uninhabited island. We find ourselves greeted, tended to, and cared for by people who are eager to teach us what we need to know.

Families provide babies with their first education. Parents, relatives, and older siblings give infants fingers and rattles to grasp, and this stimulation helps the infants learn to gauge distance and to coordinate and use their arms and hands. As time goes by, games such as patti-cake, peek-a-boo, and rolling balls back and forth serve to further that development.

Families also teach their children about the practicalities of daily life, along with its dangers (such as a hot burner) and its pleasures (such as ice cream). They teach language by giving the child a language to listen to, by practicing the sounds that construct words, and by correcting mispronunciations. Families teach a child the names of things and how to perform a variety of tasks—everything from how to dress to how to brush her teeth. Families also teach the basic rules of conduct, such as when and why to say "please" and "thank you."

Beyond the basics, families also teach more complex rules of behavior. When I was a child, I learned, for example, that sassing any adult spelled trouble, that fighting with my sisters was tolerated within limits, and that playing at the dinner table was not permitted. What I had learned from my family by the time I was five years old would make a dizzyingly long list.

When we reach school age, our intellectual education begins in earnest, and those who teach us become more specialized. Trained schoolteachers ensure that children receive a well-rounded education in subjects such as reading, writing, science, geography, history, and mathematics. As we grow older and penetrate more deeply into different spheres of knowledge, our teachers become even more specialized. We learn history from a history teacher, chemistry from a chemistry teacher, and so on. These are people who have mastered the materials that they are teaching. In college, this specialization goes even deeper, and people spend years of concentrated study in a particular field before they become qualified to teach at this level.

As we enter the virtuous stage of development—that stage that lasts the rest of our lives—to whom can we turn for instruction? People may earn a divinity or theology degree, but there are no degrees in virtue. As this is one of the most neglected and misunderstood areas of education—as well as the most critical—the next five chapters are devoted to this subject alone: the virtuous educators. We will look at Who They are, what it is They have to teach us, and what it is that makes Them especially qualified.

10

The Search

We are, by talking about virtuous capacities, at the outermost limit of what we can conceive and of what we can understand. We are standing at a horizon of sorts. In this case, the horizon is not some distant point; it is right here where we stand. Behind us are the capacities of attraction, augmentation, intelligence, and intellect. At our feet, in the here and now, is the capacity of virtue. We know what virtuous action looks like, but virtuous capacity brought to full potential mystifies us; it is beyond us and veiled. We can penetrate it a little ways, perhaps, but for the most part our full virtuous capacity lies concealed from us.

This point is also about as far as the sciences can bring us. The sciences certainly cannot tell us *how* to develop virtuously, nor can they tell us exactly what virtues are. The most they can hope to do is document the development of this capacity throughout childhood and into adulthood, but as far as "what," "how," or "why" goes, the sciences are rather useless.

As far as virtues go, I reached adulthood in a bit of a muddle. Like most folks I know, I had constructed my own working model of the universe, and virtue wasn't part of it. Like most folks' models, mine was based mostly on my observations and personal preferences. I was, at least, open-minded enough to view my model as a work in progress.

I had left the Catholic Church, without looking back, by the time I was in my late teens. At some point around the age of fourteen, I realized that I only believed in Christ because that is what I had been taught to believe. What if I had never been taught this? Had I been raised differently, would I believe differently? As I asked myself these questions, I realized that I couldn't think poorly of those who didn't believe in Christ, if that's what they had been taught. And I certainly couldn't be upset with Christ's contemporaries for not believing in Him because, unlike me, they had not been brought up to believe in Christ. They had had to figure it out for themselves. What if I had lived during the time of Christ and had had to decide for myself whether or not to believe in Him? What would I have decided? How would I have known that Jesus was who He said He was? Believing in something because it was what I had been taught seemed to be a pretty weak basis for faith. From that point on, I wondered if and how I would have recognized Christ if I had had to figure it out all on my own.

And the older I got, the less I appreciated being told I'd go to hell if I didn't believe in Christ. Threatening to punish someone if he or she doesn't cooperate is the tactic of a bully, and I knew that Christ was certainly not a bully. Christ was better than the best among us, and if He really was the Son of God, then that meant God was also better than the best among us. The threat that I would "go to hell" seemed like something a small-minded and mean-hearted person who had run out of rational explanations would say. While I had been indoctrinated into Catholicism well enough to fear the consequences if I were wrong about this—maybe God *was* mean enough to punish me for doing my best with the brain He had given me if I reached conclusions different from what I had been taught—I still couldn't help thinking it.

In addition, when I attended church, I often observed that some people fell asleep during Mass and that others left just as mean-spirited as when they had arrived. What good was going to Mass, I wondered, if it doesn't turn us into caring and loving people, even if only for a little while? Why go to Mass only to fall asleep? I knew people didn't go to Mass to sleep; they fell asleep because it was boring. It seemed to me that Mass was not actually answering their spiritual needs. It was just one more thing we had to do to avoid going to hell.

To be honest, I never felt God's presence in church. I had discovered, however, that I sometimes felt, well, *something* spiritual when I was alone in the woods. I loved to sit by the river, listening to the buzz of cicadas, inhaling the scent of dark loamy earth, and watching reflected sunlight dance in pale zigzags on green tree leaves. At times like this, a sort of hush would fall upon me—a state of receptivity, perhaps—and I would experience a deep peacefulness and a feeling of being connected with all creation. This was a feeling I had never experienced in any church or during any religious service.

As I grew older, I felt less and less of a need to bother with the sacraments, which I knew by now had not originated with Christ. I had learned that much of the Church doctrine I had been taught had not come from Christ, either. In addition, the complex authoritarian Church hierarchy is nothing short of mind-boggling and full of pompous display, and I was at a loss to explain how it had evolved from Christ's teachings or from His simple way of life. The Church looked to me like a very old man-made (and man-centered) institution that reflected little about God but much about men. The older I got, the less reason I could find to submit myself—body, mind, and soul—to it. And so, eventually, I didn't.

During this time, I was beginning to learn more about other world religions. I still have the now very beat-up and water-stained paperback book, *The Religions of Man*, by Huston Smith, that first led me to having a wider religious worldview. While I can't remember where or when I acquired it, I remember having the feeling that this book represented something very important. There was something to know about religion that I didn't yet understand. I knew I was missing something vitally important, and I wanted to find that missing piece.

Learning about other religions helped me shake off residual feelings of superiority—as well as the idea that I was favored by God for being Christian—that had been inculcated in me as I was growing up. It looked to me as if each religion was a cultural expression of essentially the same thing. What that thing was—God? Spirituality? That unnamable something I had felt in those quiet still moments in the woods?—whatever it was, it made sense to me that it would be expressed differently throughout the world.

So there I was, a young adult, rejecting Catholicism and doubtful as to Who Christ was. I even considered myself an atheist. The God I had learned about as a child was stern, ill-tempered, and indiscriminate in how punishment was meted out. He punished both guilty and innocent alike—not unlike some grade school punishments I had suffered where the whole class had to stay after school because of a few people misbehaving. Beyond this, God seemed to have an insatiable appetite for praise and admiration, and He demanded to be prayed to all the time. How could I believe in a God like that?

Now, religion can provide a moral compass of sorts, but I had learned much about the inglorious history of the Catholic Church, as well as organized religions in general. I had heard of too many acts of cruelty and violence committed in the name of religion, and even in the name of God, to believe that religion was an infallible moral guide. By the time I was in my early twenties, I had acquired a general abhorrence of organized religion and felt it was best to be as far away from it as possible.

At this point in my life, I had essentially adopted society's moral compass, which is actually pretty shabby. After all, since I had rejected religion, what could take its place to guide my virtuous development? TV? Magazines? Self-proclaimed spiritual gurus? I scanned many of them—some cursorily, some more deeply—

and found that they were all pretty much a vacuum and inevitably converged on measuring our success by the amount of our earnings and not by our ethical achievements.

This period was a spiritually and emotionally bleak time in my life, and I often woke up in the middle of the night, incredulous and disappointed at the thought that we would be born, only to live a span of years doing this or that, and then die. The overarching feeling I had during that time was hopelessness—both for the future of humanity and for my own future. Still, during this time, I couldn't shake the idea that life had to have meaning and purpose. Perhaps it was simply that while others craved things like a successful career, marriage, children, money, or status, my craving had always been for meaning.

When I was a child, I was fascinated by the stars and wanted to become an astronomer. I spent many evening hours stargazing and teaching myself the constellations. Although I gave up the idea of being an astronomer when I found out how much physics was involved, as a young adult I still found myself sometimes gazing upward toward the stars and wondering what this unimaginably immense universe was all about. I had long ago decided that I did not believe the purpose of life was merely to create more life. Certainly biological reproduction is one of life's purposes, but I didn't believe it could be life's *only* purpose, or it wouldn't have evolved along the intellectual line, which only seems to muck things up, biologically speaking. The intellect has, after all, given us the ability to pollute the air and waterways, methodically destroy ecosystems, and cause global warming, all of which threaten the health and well-being of whole species, ourselves included. From a purely biological point of view, the Earth would be better off without us.

I also knew that there had to be more to the world than what my senses told me. During those times in the woods when I felt the unfathomable, I also felt myself at the edge of what my senses could provide me. Quiet, solitary moments took me to that edge: standing at night at a lakeside, with wavelets chiming sweetly against the shore, the moon's reflection broken into shimmering dancing sparkles, with the breeze carrying watery and earthy scents. At moments like this, something in me would become very quiet, and I could feel the *something* hidden within it all. Those moments were pregnant with mystery. These scents, sights, and sounds pulled me to the edge, and if I could only figure out how to take the next step, I felt I would finally come to know that mystery. This experience can happen at any time, when I am alone in a natural setting. In order to come to grips with this kind of experience, I made up the cinnamon whistle experiment that I shared in chapter 4. It helped me rationally understand and accept the limits of what my senses could tell me. My senses could tell me some things, I came to realize, but could not give me the complete picture.

So there I was, well into the virtuous phase of development, yet I could find very little guidance on the subject of being virtuous—not that I was looking. I didn't know to look! And those moral arbiters—religious leaders—hardly provided examples of morality themselves. So many of them seemed to be in the grip of pride, anger, and intolerance that they were actually repellent to me.

And then I hit a wall.

This sounds silly now, but, having examined so many things and found them wanting, the end of the road came for me when a guy I had been dating for four months broke up with me. He had introduced me to an upper middle-class lifestyle (more accurately, middle class trying to emulate upper class), with dinners at fancy restaurants (which I loathed), skiing (which I didn't care for one way or another), and a summer vacation during which I remember eating at a dockside outdoor restaurant and being appalled at the number of pleasure boats crammed into the harbor. He was from a wealthy town, and my brief acquaintance with the culture of that town was equally appalling. Folks young and old spent much of their time drinking and partying. I was twenty-eight, and I think I was beginning to realize that I didn't actually *enjoy* partying and drinking. It definitely seemed odd that people in their forties and fifties would still want to spend their time this way. I can remember driving past a church in the downtown area and briefly wondering where I would find the Church of Our Lady of Perpetual Adolescence. Still, having little self-knowledge and even less self-esteem, I was willing to deal with it, since the one thing I really craved was to be liked and accepted.

And then he broke up with me. Just like that. I was crushed. But as I began to get over it, something new began to stir in me. I had this very strong sense that I had come full circle. I had tried doing things the way I had been taught, tried pursuing the pastimes my peers pursued. None of those things were making me happy. None of it had any meaning. I knew I had to break off from the path I was on and try something radically different. I knew that if I continued this way all I would be doing was repeating the circle. To me the choice was clear: Repeat the circle and expect more of the same, or seek guidance and find something better.

I knew I had to be very careful what guidance I chose. It had to be something better, smarter, and bigger than I. I knew it couldn't be from the pages of a magazine or anything else that American culture offers.

As a sophomore in college, I had met a fellow student who told me he was a member of the Bahá'í Faith. I can't remember a thing he told me then, but something must have impressed me because throughout my twenties, I kept a keen eye on anything about the Bahá'í Faith. At that time, Bahá'ís in Iran were being heavily persecuted by the new government of Ayatollah Khomeini (this was during the 1980s, right after the Iranian revolution), and accounts of these persecutions were often in the news. What I read about the Bahá'í Faith in those articles was very interesting to me. I learned that Bahá'ís believe in the oneness of religion, the equality of women and men, the oneness of humanity, the elimination of racial and cultural prejudice, and other high ideals. I thought, in those days, that if I ever had children I would look into this religion, for it would be a good way to raise them.

But when I was twenty-eight and I'd hit that wall, I realized that maybe I would never have children, and perhaps I needed to look into the Bahá'í Faith not for them, but for myself. If it didn't work out, I told myself, I would try other options. There were other spiritual communities, after all, who espoused tolerance and love.

So began a period of intense investigation. I was delighted to learn that independent investigation of truth is a core tenet of this religion. There is no clergy, and each person is responsible for his or her own spiritual development. Independent investigation and the lack of any clergy—both of these things were good news to me, as it meant that no one could place himself in authority over me (that is, tell me what to think) and that questions were not only welcomed but encouraged. Well, I had lots of questions. One by one, I found answers to all of them, and I also found that these answers often generated more questions.

For example, in one of Bahá'u'lláh's tablets I read:

Man is the supreme Talisman. Lack of a proper education hath, however, deprived him of that which he doth inherently possess. Through a word proceeding out of the mouth of God he was called into being; by one word more he was guided to recognize the Source of his education; by yet another word his station and destiny were safeguarded. The Great Being saith: Regard man as a mine rich in gems of inestimable value. Education can, alone, cause it to reveal its treasures, and enable mankind to benefit therefrom.[1]

I had been taught from my earliest days that I was created flawed with original sin. From a young age I was inculcated with a self-concept of being, at my inmost center, corrupt and naturally inclined toward evil. This created a self-image of being an essentially dark creature who must always struggle against her natural tendencies. To suddenly hear that I was not created tainted but was "a mine rich in gems of inestimable value" was like receiving a glass of clear, pure water after years in a parched land. Here, after hearing only revilement my whole life, I was being told that I had been created in beauty.

This was an exciting possibility. Could it be true? Bahá'u'lláh wrote that lack of a proper education had deprived me of what I inherently possessed. I wasn't sure what it was that I inherently possessed—these gems, whatever they were—but it made sense to me that humanity as a whole, myself included, was falling very far short of what we had the potential to be and do. I wondered where I would be able to find this "proper education." In another tablet I found the answer:

He [God] hath ordained that in every age and dispensation a pure and stainless Soul be made manifest in the kingdoms of earth and heaven. Unto this subtle, this mysterious and ethereal Being He hath assigned a twofold nature; the physical, pertaining to the world of matter, and the spiritual, which is born of the substance of God Himself. . . . These Essences of Detachment, these resplendent Realities are the channels of God's all-pervasive grace. Led by the light of unfailing guidance, and invested with supreme sovereignty, They are commissioned to use the inspiration of Their words, the effusions of Their infallible grace and the sanctifying breeze of Their Revelation for the cleansing of every longing heart and receptive spirit from the dross and dust of earthly cares and limitations. Then, and only then, will the Trust of God, latent in the reality of man, emerge, as resplendent as the rising Orb of Divine Revelation, from behind the veil of concealment, and implant the ensign of its revealed glory upon the summits of men's hearts.

From the foregoing passages and allusions it hath been made indubitably clear that . . . there must needs be manifested a Being, an Essence Who shall act as a Manifestation and Vehicle for the transmission of the grace of the Divinity Itself, the Sovereign Lord of all. Through the Teachings of this Daystar of Truth every man will advance and develop until he attaineth the station at which he can manifest all the potential forces with which his inmost true self hath been endowed. It is for this very purpose that in every age and dispensation the Prophets of God and His chosen Ones have appeared amongst men, and have evinced such power as is born of God and such might as only the Eternal can reveal.[2]

I had never before encountered such a description of the Prophets of God as channels of God's grace, and the idea that through Their words every longing heart and receptive soul could "manifest all the potential forces" with which their "inmost true self hath been endowed" was completely new to me.

I was certainly longing to understand what my potential forces were. And, if it had to do with me being a mine rich in gems, I wanted to find out what these gems were, too. I was, at least, open-minded about the possibilities. I would find that this open-mindedness, this condition of desire for knowledge, was a key component to my learning process. Openness lets in new things, and it's the new things and their accompanying challenges that stimulate growth.

Besides open-mindedness, the other component to the learning process, I began to understand, is the Prophets of God. I began to learn that the Prophets Bahá'u'lláh referred to—Krishna, Moses, Zoroaster, Buddha, Jesus, Muḥammad, and Bahá'u'lláh Himself—were not just any prophets, but the founders of the great world religions. He refers to these individuals by various titles—"Essences of Detachment," "Daystars of Truth," "Vehicles," "Bearers of God's Message," "Divine Physicians"—but the title I learned to refer to Them was Manifestations of God. About Them, Bahá'u'lláh wrote:

> The door of the knowledge of the Ancient Being hath ever been, and will continue forever to be, closed in the face of men. No man's understanding shall ever gain access unto His holy court. As a token of His mercy, however, and as a proof of His loving-kindness, He hath manifested unto men the Daystars of His divine guidance, the Symbols of His divine unity, and hath ordained the knowledge of these sanctified Beings to be identical with the knowledge of His own Self. Whoso recognizeth them hath recognized God. Whoso hearkeneth to their call, hath hearkened to the Voice of God, and whoso testifieth to the truth of their Revelation, hath testified to the truth of God Himself. Whoso turneth away from them, hath turned away from God, and whoso disbelieveth in them, hath disbelieved in God. Every one of them is the Way of God that connecteth this world with the realms above, and the Standard of His Truth unto every one of the kingdoms of earth and heaven. They are the Manifestations of God amidst men, the evidences of His Truth, and the signs of His glory.[3]

While I had read about the various religions and had come to see them as a human expression of either a divine reality or divine longing, I had actually given very little thought to the founders of these religions. I knew about Christ, of course, but I knew hardly anything about any of the others. Contemplating passages like the ones cited, I found myself focusing less and less on religion and more and more on the Manifestations of God. It turned out that, for me, this was a necessary adjustment to make. So, for the next few chapters, in an attitude of open-mindedness, let's turn our attention to the Manifestations of God.

11

Virtuous Educators

It is an unfortunate reality—at least for someone like me who likes to know the facts—that the further back in history we go, the less we actually know about the Manifestations of God. Very little of a historical nature survives from two thousand years ago and before. The events preserved in the historic record address the doings of kings and conquerors, not the doings of some unknown upstarts, which is how the Manifestations of God were generally viewed in Their own time.

Instead, knowledge of Them and of Their sayings and teachings was passed along orally, sometimes for generations. Perhaps, if one of Them happened to catch the interest of the right scholar, there is some mention in the historic record, but this is generally not the case. For the devout, this oral transmission is not a problem, for they feel God would safeguard it from tampering and change. For the doubtful, this oral transmission is a real problem; they note that even written records are subject to alteration.

Nevertheless, it is worth reviewing what records we do have. As most people know the story of the Founder of their own religion but have little knowledge of the Founder of any other, it is worthwhile to become acquainted with each of Them.

The following biographical portraits are in no way complete and are only intended as an introduction. I've left out, for the most part, stories of miracles, which many religious adherents use as proof of singularity. Miracles, however, are associated with each of the Manifestations of God, and so, in the interest of brevity, I have excluded them from this narration.

Krishna

It is difficult to pinpoint the timeline of Krishna's life, but He is reputed to have lived five thousand years ago. The stories that recount His life, however, are recorded in the Mahābhārata, believed to have been composed between 400 BC and 200 CE, and the Bhāgavata-Purāṇa, believed to be authored in the tenth century CE. These stories are considered to be spiritually symbolic rather than historically accurate.

According to these narratives, Krishna was born in Mathura, India, to the Yadava clan, the son of Vasudeva and Devaki. His uncle, the wicked King Kamsa of Mathura (in modern Uttar Pradésh), hearing a prophecy that he would be destroyed by a child of his sister, Devaki, set out to slay her children. Krishna was then smuggled across the Yamura River to Gokula (modern Gokul). He was then raised by Nanda, the leader of the cow herds, and his wife, Yasoda.

As a child, Krishna became known and loved for performing miracles, slaying demons, and for being something of a prankster. As a youth His flute-playing coaxed many a wife and daughter from their homes to dance with Him in the forest.

Eventually Krishna returned to Mathura with His brother, Balarama, and killed Kamsa. He then led His clan to the western coast of Kathiawar, where He established His court at Dvaraka (modern Dwarka, Gujarat).

A great war subsequently developed between two groups of cousins, the hundred Kauravas and the five Pandavas. The Pandavas had been cheated out of their share of the kingdom in a crooked dice game. Afterward, they had been told that if they lived in a forest for twelve years, and then incognito for another year, their share of the kingdom would be returned to them. After complying with these terms, they returned to make their claim, but Duryodhana (who had contrived the plot to cheat them in the first place) refused to honor the bargain. Thus the Pandavas found themselves preparing for war against their cousins.

Lord Krishna refused to participate in this war but offered His army to one side and Himself to the other side. Arjuna, a Pandava, chose Krishna. Duryodhana happily chose Krishna's army. Krishna then served as Arjuna's charioteer during the ensuing battle. When Arjuna saw that he would be fighting and even killing his own kinsmen and teachers, he quavered. Wouldn't it be better to let himself be slain, even in a just war? It is his dialogue with Krishna before this battle that is recorded in the Bhagavad Gita. This dialogue, which is considered a central text of Hinduism, covers many spiritual topics such as God, the soul, perfection, and creation.

After the war, as Krishna was returning to Dvaraka, a fight broke out among the Yadava chiefs, during which Krishna's brother and son were killed. He went into the forest to mourn His loss. A huntsman, mistaking Him for a deer, shot Him in the heel, His one vulnerable spot, and He was instantly killed.

The story of Krishna can be found in the Mahābhārata and the Bhagavata-Purāṇa. The Bhagavad Gita is also found in the Mahābhārata.[1]

Moses

Moses was born to Hebrew slaves in Egypt but was adopted as an infant by Pharaoh's daughter and raised as an Egyptian prince. Moses was born, scholars estimate, sometime during the late fourteenth and thirteenth century BCE. As a young man, He came upon an Egyptian beating a Hebrew slave. In anger, Moses struck and killed the Egyptian, and this one incident irrevocably changed the course of His life. Fearing for His life, Moses fled into the desert. There He took up residence with a priest of Midian named Jethro and married one of his daughters.

One day while tending Jethro's flock, Moses encountered a bush that was being engulfed—but not consumed—by flames. Arrested by the sight, He stopped to investigate, and, from the burning bush, He heard the voice of God:

Do not come closer. Remove your sandals from your feet, for the place on which you stand is holy ground. I am . . . the God of your father, the God of Abraham, the God of Isaac, and the God of Jacob . . .

I have marked well the plight of My people in Egypt and have heeded their outcry because of their taskmasters; yes, I am mindful of their sufferings. I have come down to rescue them from the Egyptians and to bring them out of that land to a good and spacious land, a land flowing with milk and honey . . . Now the cry of the Israelites has reached Me; moreover, I have seen how the Egyptians oppress them. Come therefore, I will send you to Pharaoh, and you shall free My people, the Israelites, from Egypt.[2]

At first Moses objected. He was a stutterer, not a man of erudition, not the man for the job at all! But when God told Him that His brother, Aaron, would speak for Him, Moses finally conceded and returned to Egypt to deliver God's demands.

Of course, Pharaoh was not about to release his labor pool. In fact, upon hearing the demands of Moses, he made conditions more difficult for the Israelites. A competition of sorts then ensued between Moses and the court magicians: staffs were turned into snakes, the Nile and all of Egypt's rivers were turned to blood, and a plague of frogs was set loose upon the lands and households. Finally, the court magicians were outdone when Moses turned dust into a plague of lice, a feat they could not match.

Even when the court magicians conceded that this was from God and not a magician's trick, Pharaoh would not relent. Next, a swarm of insects descended to ruin the land, followed by the death of all Egyptian livestock, boils on man and beast, a lethal hailstorm, and a plague of locusts. Finally, the death of all firstborn Egyptians convinced Pharaoh to release the Israelites from bondage. After their release, however, he had one more change of heart and set off after them with his army. Only when the pursuing Egyptian army had drowned in the sea were the Israelites finally free from servitude to Egypt.

Yet on their journey to the land promised by God, the Israelites discovered a foe not so easily outrun—themselves. Their forty-year trek through the desert was one of daily hardships, and food and water were scarce. While the idea of freedom from slavery can fuel many dreams, the responsibilities that had to be assumed and the attending hardships and unpredictability of such a journey soon stripped the romance from their notion of "freedom." Many Israelites began to wonder whether they hadn't been better off back in Egypt, where they'd at least had shelter and could count on dinner. Most of their complaints, doubts, stubbornness, and rebelliousness were directed at Moses. More than once, this rebelliousness ended in bloodshed.

Despite the difficulties, Moses led them and sometimes drove them forward. He not only guided their physical footsteps, He provided a moral and social compass as well in the form of laws and commands that guided behavior and restricted activities.

Many of us are most familiar with the Ten Commandments, which restricted the Israelites to the worship of one God and did away with idol worship, providing a basis for morality. Yet the laws of Moses went far beyond these and covered everything from the treatment of slaves to the resolution of disputes. Many of these laws seem strange and severe by today's standards, but we must remember that the laws were a reflection of the harshness of the existing conditions, and they probably improved or introduced rights and protections.

These laws helped solidify the Israelites into a unified nation, and they taught the Israelites how to become better individuals. The heart and soul of all of these commands is this: "Love your fellow as yourself."*

---

* Leviticus 19:18.

Moses began the journey with a loosely connected group of people and delivered a nation that would grow in strength and numbers for centuries. The land promised by God was not simply real estate but the rich culture that this ragtag band of former slaves would become. The story of the life of Moses and of His laws and commands is recorded in the Torah.

Zoroaster

The time in which Zoroaster, Founder of the Zoroastrian religion, lived, is much debated and is estimated variously between 600 BC and 1700 BC. Described as the son of an "owner of horses" and a milkmaid, He lived in the northeast of what is present-day Iran. At the age of twenty, He began to seek isolation and peace by retiring to a cave and meditating. At the age of thirty, Zoroaster began to receive visions. Contained within them was the overarching directive to lead his people to the good.

Zoroaster's teachings can be summed up as "good thoughts, good words, good deeds." Like Moses, He sought to introduce the concept of one God, known as Mazda, to a polytheistic people. There is only one God, He taught, to be worshipped in thought, word, and deed. He gave the law of God (Asha), of righteousness and spiritual purity, and of loving service to one's fellow. Zoroaster taught that a person can live a good life only by fighting a constant battle against evil. The power of intelligence gives each person the ability to choose between good and evil and to understand the challenges of living the good life. Intelligence also allows us to understand the consequences of evil.

At first, only one cousin listened to Zoroaster's message. For some years, Zoroaster and His cousin traveled from village to village trying to find someone who would listen to his message. The existing clergy, described as generally corrupt, opposed Him at every turn.

Then Kavi Vishtaspa, king of Batria (present-day Afghanistan), invited Zoroaster to his court to tell him of His new doctrine. For three days, Zoroaster preached, eliciting jealousy in some courtiers. Determined to discredit Him, they hid bones, human hair, and similar things under His pillow, swearing the innkeeper to silence under threat of death. Then in open court, they accused Zoroaster of being a black magician and produced their evidence. The angry king had Zoroaster imprisoned.

At the same time, Vishtaspa's favorite horse, Aspa Siha, became ill and collapsed in pain. None of the physicians could cure him. When Zoroaster heard of this event, He sent word to Vishtaspa that He would cure the horse.

Vishtaspa gave his permission, but before Zoroaster would cure Aspa Siha, He made four demands. First, the king must accept Zoroaster's new religion. Vishtaspa agreed. Zoroaster stroked one leg of Aspa Siha, and immediately the leg was healed.

Next, Zoroaster asked be taken to Queen Hutoxshi to explain His doctrine to her. This was allowed, and the queen gladly accepted the new religion. Zoroaster then healed the second leg of the horse.

Next, He asked that the Crown Prince, Asfandiar, swear allegiance to the new faith and spread it abroad. This was done, and Zoroaster healed the third leg.

Finally, He asked that the innkeeper be brought before the king to tell where the materials under His pillow had come from. The innkeeper confessed and pointed out the guilty parties. Zoroaster intervened on behalf of the courtiers, whom Vishtaspa had ordered to be beheaded. Instead, they were banished from court and the city and forced to make their own way in the world. By this time, Aspa Siha's cure was complete.

From that point the religion spread quickly, despite great resistance from the priestly class. Zoroaster was in His mid-seventies when He was assassinated while at prayer in the Temple of Balkh (Kabul). The surviving scripture attributed to Him is the Gathas, in which He identifies with the oppressed herdsman, the poor, and the downtrodden. The Gathas were memorized by His followers and passed along orally until transcribed circa 400 CE.

Buddha

The date of Buddha's birth is estimated to be 536 BC. His early life was one of luxury and sensual diversion, for He was born into royalty, sheltered, protected, and pampered. The choicest foods, beautiful dancing girls, the most thrilling hunt—in short, anything that could give him pleasure—was His for the asking.

Nevertheless, even such a protected one as this young prince could not remain forever ignorant of the harsher realities of life. Sometime in His early twenties the awareness of the existence of disease, hardship, old age, and death was suddenly thrust upon Him.

Instead of fleeing back into diversionary forgetfulness, He became preoc- cupied with the existence of suffering and the purpose of life. At the age of twenty-nine, He decided to leave home and devote His life to solving these mysteries.

Shortly before He left, the god Nara, described as the lord of this world and the god of sin, greed, and death, appeared to tempt Him. *Become a cakkavati, a world ruler,* Nara urged, *and put an end to the world's suffering through benevolent government.*

But Buddha knew very well that suffering is not a condition that can be overcome by force, and He refused Nara's offer. One night shortly thereafter, He set out, shaving His head and exchanging His clothes for those of a poor passerby. And so began His search for peace of mind and for that which never grows old, wears out, or dies.

It was popularly held at that time that the self is full of cravings. When these cravings—whether needs or desires—are denied, then suffering is born. Abandon the self, therefore, and suffering is vanquished. Certain disciplines had been developed that promised enlightenment through self-abandonment, and for the next six years, Buddha attempted to find enlightenment through these methods. He quickly mastered various types of yoga and meditation, reputed to liberate the skilled practitioner from the self.

While He did find release, it turned out to be only temporary, and His desires and needs inevitably returned. Next, with five other mendicants, He practiced the life of an ascetic, denying Himself food and drink, sleeping on a mattress of spikes, and avoiding all company. After a time He grew thin and gaunt, His body and mind weakening. He realized that this path, too, was ineffective, for while it was not only wearing out His body, it was also making Him too weak to meditate effectively, and it actually intensified His needs and desires. At that point He abandoned the practice of asceticism, concluding that the extremes of a life of both luxury and deprivation are inappropriate and that a moderate lifestyle is preferable.

His efforts to acquire peace of mind and enlightenment through conventional means had failed Him. Determined to acquire insight into the ultimate reality of things, He sat one day beneath a fig tree and began to meditate. There He sat, hour after hour, passing from stage to stage, from one spiritual experience to another, until finally He found enlightenment. At that moment He became awakened, understanding fully all that is and all that concerns life and its purpose.

From that point onward, He began to teach, sharing His knowledge in order to lead others to the truth. His reputation spread, and He became widely known for both His intellectual penetration into abstruse matters and His boundless compassion—a man who showed equal respect to kings and outcasts alike.

Buddha taught the principles of the "Middle Way," which avoids the extremes of sensual indulgence and asceticism. The Middle Way requires an understanding of the Four Noble Truths: that life involves suffering; that suffering is caused by desire and clinging to worldly things, which by their very nature are impermanent; that by destroying desire we may become free of sorrow; and that in order to eliminate attachment one must practice the Noble Eightfold Path.

The Noble Eightfold Path consists of right belief and right intention (one must gain insight into the truth about life and develop a motivation based on compassion); right speech, right action, and right livelihood (one must live kindly and morally, acknowledging the importance of what one does as well as what one says, and apply ethics to both public and private life); and right effort, right mindfulness, and right meditation (one must train the mind). It is in this manner—as one strives to achieve perfect self-control, unselfishness, knowledge, and enlightenment—that anger, passion, and sin are rejected.

Buddha traveled the surrounding country for the next forty-five years, resting for three months out of the year, when monsoons made travel difficult. Thousands responded to His message, which made spiritual enlightenment, formerly the jealously guarded province of the priestly Brahmin class, accessible to all. He passed away at age eighty after a brief illness. His teachings were memorized and passed along orally for three hundred years until recorded in the first century BCE and are known as "The Pali Canon" and the Tipitaka (the Three Baskets).

Jesus Christ

Jesus was the son of a Jewish carpenter and, like His father, was also a carpenter by trade. The Gospels speak mostly of the events during the final three years of His life, and very little information about His earlier life is available. At this point in history, the Jews had long been ruled over and oppressed by the Romans. Yet their hope for liberation in the form of a Messiah sent by God ran high.

John the Baptist was a wandering teacher whose mission was to prepare his listeners for the appearance of this Messiah. John practiced immersion baptism, which involved briefly submerging a person in a body of water to symbolize the purification and washing away of the individual's sins. This act always marked a turning point in the lives of those who were baptized, who then committed themselves to live better lives from that point forward.

When Jesus came to John for baptism, John balked, declaring that it was he who needed to be baptized by Jesus. Yet Jesus insisted, and John relented and baptized Him. As the gospel of Matthew states:

And Jesus, when he was baptized, went up straightway out of the water: and, lo, the heavens were opened unto him, and he saw the Spirit of God descending like a dove, and lighting upon him: And lo a voice from heaven, saying, This is my beloved Son, in whom I am well pleased.[3]

This was the first intimation of the divine mission that had been entrusted to Him. Needing to prepare Himself further, Jesus withdrew to the desert to fast for forty days and nights.

There He lived alone, except for the companionship of wild beasts. And there He was tempted three times by Satan. First Satan tempted the fasting Jesus to turn stones into bread to eat. Jesus refused, stating that man cannot live by bread alone but only by the word of God. Then he took Jesus to the top of the temple, telling Him that if He jumped off, God would send angels to catch him. Again, Jesus refused. He would not use His powers to play cheap tricks or test God. Finally, Satan offered Jesus dominion over the world. Jesus again refused, making it clear that His dominion was not an earthly one. Finally the rebuked Satan departed with a promise to return at a more opportune time.

As soon as Jesus returned from the desert, He sought out twelve men who would be His apostles, and He began to spread His message. Jesus identified Himself with the outcasts of society such as the poor and downtrodden. For Him, social class and wealth meant nothing. He loved each person without judgment and with a deep compassion.

The Jewish temple, a symbol of the heart of Jewish culture, had become a center of commerce. Its activities had deteriorated into a system of rules, duties, and obligations to be met. Jesus pointed out the hypocrisy behind these ritualized and public spiritual practices, along with many people's accompanying fixation on the letter of the law. He also attacked the businesses that had sprung up around the temple, where money-changers did business and animals were sold for sacrifice.

Obedience to the letter of the law was no substitute for true spiritual devotion, He told His listeners. Devotion to God depends solely on each person's private relationship with God, He explained, and not on public displays. Material wealth and position in society is of little consequence. What matters is purity of mind and heart, and faith in God, which must be demonstrated through action. Jesus challenged His listeners to express their spiritual devotion through acts of compassion, such as feeding the hungry and caring for the sick.

Jesus disrupted people's complacency by proclaiming that the life of the spirit was not the domain of priests but rather of God, Who loves each of His creatures dearly. Each individual—born high or low—was able to receive this love and to be reborn, animated with its spirit. When someone showed this kind of spiritual devotion, he would become a lover of humanity, even to the degree of loving his worst enemies. This love was true proof of faith and was pleasing to God, and it was the path to salvation and eternal life.

Jesus spoke to the multitudes in parables that were abstruse yet rich in meaning for those who made an effort to understand them. He drew from everyday scenarios and used them to illustrate the spiritual principles that should inform people's lives, and He explained their relationship with God and assured them of God's love for them. The spiritual principles that Christ spoke of had nothing to do with the conventions of the day such as rituals or sacrifices.

In fact, much of what Jesus taught flew in the face of convention and contemporary interpretation of the law. When He healed people on the Sabbath, for example, Jesus was accused of breaking Mosaic law. He associated with the lower classes of society, such as the poor, and associated with women, even a prostitute. He told the wealthy they were better off inviting the poor to their tables rather than their peers. Through His teachings and deeds, Jesus began to slowly loosen the grip of the Pharisees and scribes over the general population.

The society in which Jesus lived was one in which positions and trades were inherited. For example, the son of a priest would become a priest, the son of a carpenter would become a carpenter, and so on. It was a society consumed with the letter of the law, having codified all the steps necessary for being favored by God and living the spiritual life. By contrast, Jesus taught that this kind of inheritance and adherence to such laws was not as important as one's relationship with God. This idea was attractive to some but unwelcome to others. Jesus, of course, had no formal religious training or background (not to mention no social connections), and He was hardly qualified in the eyes of the Pharisees to challenge the status quo. The response of the populace to Him, however, was impossible to ignore, for wherever He went He attracted crowds.

Eventually, He was arrested. Perhaps the authorities resented His disrupting normal temple activity, perhaps they were alarmed at the crowds who gathered to hear Him speak, or perhaps they saw Him as someone who was stirring up the masses. In the end, He was condemned as a false prophet and sentenced to death for His claim to be the Messiah and the Son of God, a claim the authorities believed blasphemous.

At the age of thirty-three, only three years after His ministry had begun, He was executed by the Roman method of crucifixion. His life and teachings are recorded in the Gospels of Matthew, Mark, Luke, and John.

Muḥammad

Muḥammad was born in the land of Arabia, circa 570 CE, among a people often described as proud, passionate, and violent. Blood feuds and tribal wars erupted at the slightest provocation. A man's supreme goal was to acquire wealth, and many people spent their lives gambling and drinking.

Women were considered to be of so little value that many people would bury their infant daughters alive. Men ran the society and were able to take as many wives as they could afford.

There was little in the way of law, and the poor and weak were ruthlessly subjugated by a corrupt power structure. The people paid homage to a variety of idols that had been placed around the Kaaba, which was located in Mecca. The Kaaba was the holiest shrine in Arabia, and during the time of Abraham, it had been a place where only God was worshipped. By Muḥammad's time, however, the worship of idols had become commonplace, and 360 idols—one for each day of the year, according to the calendar at the time—had been placed around the Kaaba.

Orphaned before the age of two, Muḥammad was first raised by His grandfather, chief of the ruling clan in Mecca, until He was eight years old. Upon His grandfather's death, He was taken in to be raised by an uncle. Despite the status of His grandfather and clan, Muḥammad was not Himself wealthy and went to work at a young age—first tending herds, then keeping a shop and going on caravan expeditions. He was known early to be a wise, peaceful man, and He was called al-Amín (the Trustworthy).

At the age of twenty-five He went to work for a rich widow, Khadijah, as a trader. Although fifteen years his senior, Khadijah fell in love with Muḥammad, and they married. It was a very happy marriage, and Muḥammad was now a wealthy man.

Still, it was impossible for Him to ignore the degenerate moral abyss into which His fellow countrymen had sunk. As time went by, Muḥammad became more introspective and often withdrew to the peace and solitude of the hills surrounding Mecca, particularly a cave on Mount Hira.

At some point during this time, the angel Gabriel appeared to Him bearing a tablet. Three times the angel told Him to read the tablet, and three times Muḥammad replied that He could not read. Then the content of the tablet burst upon Him:

Recite thou, in the name of thy Lord who created;—
Created man from clots of blood:—
Recite thou! For thy Lord is the most Beneficent,
Who hath taught the use of pen;—
Hath taught Man that which he knoweth not.[4]

This was the first of the revelations that would continue for twenty-three years. Muḥammad at first doubted His own sanity, and His wife, Khadijah, was the first to believe that He had been chosen by God to be His messenger. She would be His most loyal supporter and helpmate until the end of her life.

The revelations continued to come to Muḥammad. He commanded people to believe only in the one true God and to abandon the worship of idols. He declared that in the sight of God all men were equal, forbade injustice, and warned of punishment for those who disbelieved and rejected these commands.

When Muḥammad relayed these revelations, at first He found few believers. After all, believing in these revelations would require someone to detach himself from the licentious pastimes so enjoyed by the citizens of Mecca. Instead, Muḥammad's teachings about social justice and equality only served to rankle and annoy members of the upper class.

Over time, however, the numbers of those who believed His message increased until the aristocracy of Mecca began to feel that Muḥammad's teachings were a threat to their own religion, which was also the source of their livelihood. As custodians of the Kaaba, they relied on the trade brought from the stream of pilgrims.

In response, they attempted to silence Muḥammad, first with bribes, then with threats. Yet He persisted in delivering the message God had given Him. His life was protected only because the murder of a member of the ruling clan would be answered with swift, brutal, and bloody retaliation. However, He became the target of continual harassment. He was constantly subjected to verbal attacks and was accused of practicing magic, a charge that was calculated to provoke disgust and abhorrence in these superstitious people. He was sometimes struck, had ashes thrown over him, and had thorns scattered in his path.

Many of His followers, who were poor and powerless, were arrested and tortured in fruitless attempts to force them to recant their newfound faith. Despite these persecutions, Muḥammad continued to denounce idol worship and call the people to worship one God and obey His command.

Years of extreme hardship followed, including a three-year boycott that forbade marriage or trade with Muḥammad and His relatives. This boycott is believed to have hastened the death of Muḥammad's beloved Khadijah, who died shortly after it ended. Then Muḥammad's uncle, Abu-Tálib, who had extended his protection to Muḥammad, died. His successor, Abú-Lahab, shortly thereafter withdrew all protection from Muḥammad and disowned Him. Muḥammad decided it was time to leave Mecca. Yet where could He go? Most people still scoffed at His message.

During the pilgrim season of 620, Muḥammad met with some men from Yathrib, who accepted His message. The following year, twelve men traveled from Yathrib to meet Him. The year after that, seventy-two men and three women came from Yathrib to meet Him. Muḥammad was promised protection and that they would stand by Him at all costs. Muḥammad first sent His followers to Yathrib, and then, despite being closely watched, managed His own escape shortly thereafter.

In Yathrib, renamed Medina after His arrival, the Muslims were treated as honored guests and given shelter. Muḥammad was quickly appointed to a leadership role. He worked to unite Medina, a city that was divided into five disparate and contentious clans, two of which were Jewish. This unification was not a bloodless transition, but finally an alliance was forged between the various tribes. It was the first ever such alliance between these factions.

Within the year, Muḥammad had become head of Medina, whose Muslim population was growing rapidly. Despite His status, He chose to live in an ordinary clay house, mend His own clothes, milk His own goats, and be available to all people, whether of high or low birth. He ruled with enough sternness to keep order, and He did not hesitate to punish the guilty. However, whenever any injury was directed toward Himself, He was quick to forgive, showing mercy even to His sworn enemies.

Peace, however, was not to come easily. So highly valued were blood ties and kinship to the Meccans that the defection of Muḥammad and His followers to Yathrib was seen as an insult that demanded revenge. Consequently the Meccans attacked Medina, and although they outnumbered the Medinians, the Medinians routed and defeated them. The Meccans attacked again the next year, and this time the Medinians suffered great losses. Two years would pass, however, before the Meccans returned to Medina a third time to lay siege to the city. This siege failed, and within three years Muḥammad led a large band of followers to Mecca and captured it without bloodshed. Once He had taken control of Mecca, Muḥammad destroyed the idols that had desecrated the Kaaba and made it a place of worship for the one true God. Afterward, Muḥammad granted amnesty to His enemies, and many of them became Muslims.

Muḥammad died in 632 after leading a pilgrimage to the Kaaba. Before He died, he gave a final speech urging kindness and respect among the people, especially toward women.

Muḥammad was stern in punishing criminals but always forgave His personal enemies. He taught patience, forgiveness, and kindness to animals, and instructed His followers to give alms to the poor. He taught people to love the next world, describing this physical world as a vapor in the desert. He taught the existence of one universal God, the immortality of the soul, and accountability for actions. He dramatically curtailed aggression, forbade vengeance of blood and blood feuds, and permitted war only in self-defense and under well-defined conditions. He forbade drinking, gambling, usury, and all forms of vice, and He greatly restricted polygamy. He encouraged the abolition of slavery and set an example by freeing His own slaves. He exhorted Muslim men to treat women with respect and increased women's rights in a variety of ways, including giving wives the same property rights as their husbands, along with rights to alimony.

As Muḥammad revealed His verses, they were written down on anything close by: palm leaves, leather, stone, and shoulder blades of sheep. Six hundred and fifty revealed verses were collected and recorded in the Koran. The first Koran was compiled within three years after His death.

Bahá'u'lláh

Bahá'u'lláh was born on November 12, 1817, into a noble family in Persia. He became known at an early age for His intelligence, eloquence, and knowledge, as well as for His great benevolence.

When Bahá'u'lláh came of age, He refused to pursue a career that would ensure status and wealth. Instead, He expended His own resources on caring for the needy. In a society where compassion toward the impoverished and suffering had become virtually nonexistent, Bahá'u'lláh's unusual generosity caused Him to become widely known as "the Father of the Poor."

When He was twenty-seven, Bahá'u'lláh learned of a new religion that promoted spiritual and moral reformation of society, brotherly love, kindness to children, courtesy, elimination of prejudice, education, useful sciences, and the upliftment of women and the poor. The Founder of this new religion called Himself the Báb* (Arabic for "Gate" or "Door"), Who proclaimed that He was

* The Báb is considered a Prophet of God in His own right, and Bahá'ís refer to the Báb and Bahá'u'lláh as the "Twin Manifestations." For purposes of brevity, however, I am focusing this narrative on the life of Bahá'u'lláh. To learn more about the Báb, refer to H. M. Balyuzi's *The Báb: The Herald of the Day of Days* (Oxford: George Ronald, 1973).

the portal through which a greater man than He would soon appear. The Promised One would fulfill the prophecies of every world religion and would usher in an age of peace and justice. Bahá'u'lláh immediately embraced this new religion and set about spreading its message.

As the new religion gained adherents, the authorities reacted with ruthless fury. Over the next several years, at the hands of mobs, armies, and executioners, twenty thousand men, women, and children were tortured and put to death, and in 1850, the Báb Himself was executed by a firing squad.

Bahá'u'lláh was somewhat protected by His rank as a nobleman, but He was still subject to harassment and arrest. In one instance He was arrested with some fellow Bábís. After a failed attempt by some mullás* and siyyids† to incite a mob to murder the incarcerated Bábís, it was decided to bastinado His companions. The bastinado was a painful ordeal in which a person's feet would be repeatedly whipped, often until they bled. Bahá'u'lláh, however, insisted on taking the punishment in place of His companions. The exchange was reluctantly granted, and Bahá'u'lláh suffered the blows of the bastinado, thus sparing His friends.

Two years later, after a half-crazy Bábí attempted to assassinate the shah, a new wave of retribution spread to engulf countless innocent Bábís. This wave also engulfed Bahá'u'lláh, Who was now a well-known leader of the new faith. He was forced to walk many miles, beaten and bastinadoed, and cast into a dark, filthy dungeon notoriously known as the "Black Pit." With no drainage or removal of wastes, its atmosphere was thick with rot and decay.

Bahá'u'lláh's feet were placed in stocks, and He was fettered to five other Bábís by a 110-pound chain fastened around his neck. Each day, a Bábí was taken out to be tortured and executed. Under these most hopeless of circumstances, Bahá'u'lláh first became aware of His future calling. He describes it in these words:

One night, in a dream, these exalted words were heard on every side: "Verily, We shall render Thee victorious by Thyself and by Thy Pen. Grieve Thou not for that which hath befallen Thee, neither be Thou afraid, for Thou art in safety. Erelong will God raise up the treasures of the earth—men who will aid Thee through Thyself and through Thy Name, wherewith God hath revived the hearts of such as have recognized Him."[5]

---

* Muslim priest.

† A title given to descendants of Muḥammad.

Four months later, the Russian consul came to Bahá'u'lláh's aid by extending the protection of Russia to Him. The Russian consul threatened retaliation by the Russian government if any harm should come to Bahá'u'lláh. The Persian authorities then found it expeditious to grant Bahá'u'lláh's freedom.

Although extremely debilitated and barely able to walk, Bahá'u'lláh was immediately banished to Baghdad in neighboring Iraq. Many members of His family—including His pregnant wife, Navváb, His young children, and a few loyal companions—accompanied Him into exile on a hazardous three-month midwinter journey on horses and mules across snow-swept mountains.

In Baghdad, Bahá'u'lláh set about revitalizing the remnants of the Bábí community. His half-brother Mírzá Yaḥyá, who had earlier fled in disguise to Baghdad, had until then acted as nominal leader of the Bábís. Jealous of Bahá'u'lláh's rising prestige and emerging leadership, he began to spread rumors questioning His character and capabilities. As these criticisms circulated, conflict broke out among the Bábís, the atmosphere turned contentious, and the Bábí community began to disintegrate.

This disunity and rancor was a source of great anguish for Bahá'u'lláh. Finally, on April 10, 1854, He decided to remove Himself as a cause of ill-feeling among the Bábís and left Baghdad for the mountains of Kurdistan. He did not intend to return.

In Kurdistan He lived a secluded life, sometimes in a simple stone structure atop a mountain or sometimes in a cave. Alone in the mountain wilderness, He communed with God. Periodically He would visit a nearby town to buy supplies and would sit at a coffeehouse and discuss philosophy with anyone who wished to listen.

Soon His reputation grew. Almost two years after His departure, when His family heard rumors of a wise man living in Kurdistan, they knew it must be Bahá'u'lláh. An emissary was immediately sent to beg Him to return, for the Bábí Faith was on the verge of extinction. With great reluctance, Bahá'u'lláh agreed to return.

Bahá'u'lláh's leadership revived the Bábí community. Despite being a known exile, Bahá'u'lláh's prestige increased, and the leaders of Baghdad often sought Him out to answer perplexing questions. Suspicion was gradually replaced with trust and respect, and the Bábí Faith began to grow once again. Finally, Bahá'u'lláh's popularity proved too much for certain dignitaries, who set about forcing His removal from the city. In 1863, fearing a resurgence of the new religion, the authorities ordered Bahá'u'lláh to move to Constantinople.

The news of Bahá'u'lláh's imminent departure spread through the populace. To accommodate all who wished to visit Him and pay their respects, He went to a nearby rose garden, which had been offered to Him for just that purpose. There He remained for twelve days, receiving visitors and making His farewells. While He sojourned in that garden, He announced to His companions that He was not only the Promised One foretold by the Báb, but also the Promised One foretold in all the world's scriptures. This announcement brought great joy to the grieving companions who were about to be separated from Him. On the twelfth day, Bahá'u'lláh's family joined Him, and they departed together. Grieving crowds lined the roadway, weeping inconsolably as they watched this much-beloved personage leaving them.

Bahá'u'lláh stayed in Constantinople for only three and a half months until the Ottoman sultan, fearful of His growing prestige, exiled Bahá'u'lláh to Adrianople (modern-day Edirne, Turkey). There He spent the next four and a half years. During this time, His half-brother Mírzá Yaḥyá began to plot to murder Bahá'u'lláh. He smeared His teacup with poison, and its effects caused Bahá'u'lláh to become severely ill for weeks and left Him with a shaking hand for the rest of His life. At another time, Mírzá Yaḥyá poisoned the well used by Bahá'u'lláh's family, making them all ill for some time.

During His time in Adrianople, Bahá'u'lláh began to write tablets to the leaders of the world. The list of recipients included Napoleon III, Queen Victoria, Pope Pius IX, Náṣiri'd-Dín Sháh (the king of Persia), Kaiser Wilhelm I of Germany, and the Emperor Franz Joseph of Austria. In these tablets Bahá'u'lláh proclaimed His mission and warned the leaders of approaching political and social upheavals. He called upon them to turn their resources and energies toward the welfare of their people and the establishment of just government, and He urged them to form a commonwealth of nations in which they could act collectively against war and thereby ensure international peace. However, most of these leaders quickly dismissed Bahá'u'lláh's letters and ignored His call for peace and justice.

As in Baghdad, Bahá'u'lláh's prestige rose, and the highest dignitaries and divines once again sought His presence. Others, however, remained His bitter enemies. Mírzá Yaḥyá continuously fed lies about Bahá'u'lláh to these enemies, and soon they plotted to exile Him yet again. The breaking point came when Mírzá Yaḥyá falsely charged that Bahá'u'lláh was involved with Bulgarian revolutionaries—a charge that gave His enemies the excuse they were looking for.

Early one morning, soldiers arrived and surrounded His home, and Bahá'u'lláh was made a prisoner under house arrest. The next day, all of the Bahá'ís were arrested, and their goods were confiscated and sold off for half their value. Eight days later, Bahá'u'lláh, His family, and a few companions were forced into their final exile—this time to a penal colony in 'Akká, Palestine (now 'Akká, Israel), where only the worst criminals were sent. Bahá'u'lláh's enemies assumed that His influence would finally be extinguished there, for He would surely succumb to disease in this pestilential place.

They arrived on August 31, 1868. Confined to prison barracks, with only the most brackish water available, the exiles quickly contracted malaria and dysentery, and three soon died. Charges against the Bahá'ís of atheism, terrorism, and heresy were read out at mosques, and residents were warned not to associate with them. Sentiment against them was so poisoned that any Bahá'í appearing in public risked being pursued and harassed. Even the children risked being pelted with stones.

For a year the isolation of the Bahá'ís was strictly enforced, yet as time went by, local officials, who were coming to respect Bahá'u'lláh, began to disregard the orders. The locals, who found in the Bahá'ís upright conduct and great gentleness, gradually forgot their animosity and prejudice.

In 1870 the prisoners were removed from the barracks, which were now needed by troops, and eventually adequate housing was found for all. Although the edict that Bahá'u'lláh and the Bahá'ís be kept in strict confinement was never rescinded, it became a piece of meaningless paper, quite forgotten. However, attacks still flared up, ensuring that the exiles never felt free from harassment or even safe with their lives.

Bahá'u'lláh lived in 'Akká for nine years until a local official beseeched Him to move to a house outside of the city, where His health could be restored in the serenity of the countryside.

Bahá'u'lláh continued to reveal tablets during the final years of His life. These tablets were a combination of discourses on spiritual teachings and social directives. He revealed innumerable prayers and other writings, instructing Bahá'ís to pray at least once a day and to read the sacred writings in the morning and in the evening. At the core of all His teachings was His directive to "possess a pure, kindly and radiant heart."[6]

He taught that there is only one God and one religion that has been progressively revealed by successive Manifestations of God throughout the ages. He made it the responsibility of every individual to seek out truth for himself or herself and not to blindly follow the leadership of any other person. He promoted the equality of women and men, universal education, and the elimination of the extremes of wealth and poverty. He taught that science and religion must be in harmony and replaced confrontation with consultation as a means to solve disputes. He taught that humanity is one and that loyalty to the human race must supersede nationalistic ideologies. Indeed, world unity is inevitable, He said, but the path humanity has chosen has ensured that this unity will only be achieved after much suffering and despair.

Bahá'u'lláh died after a brief illness in 1892, still a prisoner in Palestine. Many of His original tablets are preserved at the Bahá'í World Center, in Haifa, Israel. Published tablets can be found in a number of books, including *The Kitáb-i-Íqán* (The Book of Certitude), *The Kitáb-i-Aqdas* (The Most Holy Book), *Epistle to the Son of the Wolf, The Hidden Words, Gleanings from the Writings of Bahá'u'lláh, Tablets of Bahá'u'lláh, The Summons of the Lord of Hosts,* and *Gems of Divine Mysteries.*

12

. . . And Do Good

As we read through the biographies of the Manifestations of God, we begin to get the picture that these were not ordinary men. They may be separated by great gulfs of time and culture, but Their stories have much in common.

Their early lives appear normal enough, but in each of Their lives, a moment occurs in which everything changes. For Buddha, it was His experience under the fig tree. For Moses, it was His encounter with the Burning Bush. For Christ, it was the appearance of the Holy Spirit in the form of a dove. For Muḥammad, it was His encounter with the angel Gabriel. For Bahá'u'lláh, it was His time in prison in the Black Pit.

Whatever those experiences signified for each of Them personally, it signaled the beginning of active ministries in which each came to be known for embodying every human perfection. They had no teacher, no one from whom They learned, and yet They possessed unsurpassed knowledge and wisdom. Even under the most hopeless and dire conditions, They remained incorruptible and undeviating in purpose. Each can be described as intellectually acute, possessing penetrating insight, compassionate, loving, humble, forbearing, virtuous in conduct, and fearless in His attack on corrupt religious institutions and meaningless adherence to ritualized ceremonies. They did not bow to kings, nor did They exalt themselves over the disenfranchised and poor. They treated everyone—men and women, rich and poor, of every ethnicity and social stratum—with equal respect. They did not judge others by wealth, race, gender, social status, fame, or education. Instead They judged others by their character. Each had the capacity to look past earthly trappings and into the very heart—exposed and unadorned—of every person.

In the ordinary course of events, those who impact and influence the lives of their contemporaries are wealthy, command great armies, rule over kingdoms, or control vast resources. This is in contrast to those Manifestations of God Who were born into wealth but Who willingly left it behind and lived in poverty.

Yet They commanded, and continue to command, an unparalleled love and loyalty. They influenced, and continue to influence, the thoughts and behavior of countless people. They are remembered, praised, and honored long after great kings and generals have been forgotten.

Bahá'u'lláh calls the Manifestations of God "channels of God's all-pervasive grace," through Whose teachings every person "will advance and develop until he attaineth the station at which he can manifest all the potential forces with which his inmost true self hath been endowed."[1]

Thus I had found, when I began to study Bahá'u'lláh's teachings, the source of virtuous education. It would take me some time to truly comprehend that my continuing development depended upon what I could learn from Bahá'u'lláh.

Looking back now, from the age of fifty, I can see that when I was twenty-eight and felt that I had come full-circle, I truly *had* come full-circle. As I was no longer developing virtuously, my personal development had stalled. In one sense, I was still learning throughout my twenties. I was learning by experiencing the essential emptiness of much-vaunted pastimes and goals. I knew by the age of twenty-eight that mainstream culture could offer me nothing that would lead to abiding happiness. I felt unhappy, uncomfortable, disillusioned, and dissatisfied, and I knew that something had to change. This unhappiness pushed me to examine the course of my life and find another path. Had I gone on as before, with my behavior and goals unchanged, my developmental spiral would have become circular instead. By turning to Bahá'u'lláh, I avoided this repetition, and the entrapping circle reopened to a spiral. My life has never been the same since.

I don't want to give the impression that, from that point forward I totally avoided mistakes and missteps. Certainly not. I am human, after all, and I cannot bypass the developmental process. I've made plenty of huge mistakes and always will. But I was learning how to approach myself—along with my shortcomings, insecurities, and problems—in new ways. I had become engaged in the process of forging my character, of learning how to make my words and deeds conform to each other. I struggle with this still, every day, yet the fruits of these efforts are so rich and rewarding that the longer I engage in the process, the more committed I become.

I also found, even as I was connecting with Bahá'u'lláh, that I was reconnecting with Christ in a deeper and more profound way than I ever had in my youth. I was gaining a new understanding of His unique station. In fact, I found myself connecting with all of the founders of the world's great religions.

Bahá'u'lláh says that the Manifestations of God are "commissioned to use the inspiration of Their words"[2] to teach us how to manifest our potential. I wanted to find for myself that common thread—the words They each use to teach us— between the scriptures. I could no longer be satisfied with what anyone had to say on the subject, except for the Manifestations of God. I wanted to hear Their own words and no one else's. And so began my search for the scriptures attributed to each.

Some scripture, of course, was easy to locate. Bibles can be found everywhere in this part of the world, and it is only in the Gospels that I was able to find Christ's own words. I took a trip to a Jewish bookstore to find the Torah, which contains the teachings and laws of Moses. I knew the Torah was part of the Old Testament, but I felt it was important to have the Jewish Torah. I also found various translations of the Koran in my local bookstore. I learned from some internet research that the Gathas were attributed to Zoroaster, and I was able to find a translation, printed in India, and order it through my local bookstore. I had a harder time finding scripture attributed to the Buddha, but after some searching, I learned of the Tipitaka,which is comprised of more volumes than I presently have a mental grasp of. At the time of my research I could only find some partial translations, but that situation is improving. Perhaps all volumes will soon be available in English. The Bhagavad Gita, which I learned was attributed to Krishna, I already owned.

I won't make you go through the same search. For the interested seeker, here is the list of scriptures I used to learn as much as possible about each Manifestation of God:

Krishna—Bhagavad Gita
Moses—The Torah
Zoroaster—The Gathas
Gautama Buddha—Tipitaka (Triple Baskets)
Jesus Christ—Gospels of Matthew, Mark, Luke, and John
Muḥammad—The Koran
Bahá'u'lláh—The Hidden Words, The Kitáb-i-Aqdas, and The Kitáb-i-Íqán. Other books available containing the writings of Bahá'u'lláh are *Gleanings from the Writings of Bahá'u'lláh, Epistle to the Son of the Wolf, Tablets of Bahá'u'lláh, The Summons of the Lord of Hosts,* and *Gems of Divine Mysteries.* Many more tablets of Bahá'u'lláh that have not yet been translated

into English and published are housed in the archives of the Bahá'í World Center in Haifa, Israel.

As I acquired these scriptures I began to study them, and I soon plunged into utter confusion.

The problem, I discovered, was that a large part of these scriptures are directed toward a particular society at a particular time in history. As a result, they address the immediate needs of the people at that time. I found that social ordinances and laws vary widely from book to book, that they are culturally specific, and that they really make sense only in their respective historical and cultural contexts. I was puzzled and sometimes even horrified by the seemingly cruel nature of the laws and directives that addressed subjects such as slavery, crops, treatment of wives and daughters, as well as rites, rituals, and animal sacrifices.

My response to this confusion was to go into "desert island" mode. This is a way I have of clearing my mind of my prejudices and assumptions, and helps me accept, and even welcome, a feeling of confusion. I had come up with it years earlier when I had decided I wanted to read only what Christ had said in the Gospels. I call this "reading the red parts" because, in my Bible, the words attributed to Christ are printed in red.

To prepare myself for reading the red parts, I pretended that I had long been stranded on a desert island, far away from modern civilization and Western culture. I pretended I hadn't been taught any cultural values, such as how wonderful my country is, the importance of money, or the superiority of capitalism as an economic system. On this island, I hadn't been raised in a religion or taught anything about religion at all. I knew nothing of races, cultures, or nations. I knew only what I found on that island: the sand, the trees, the ocean, the fish, the birds, and the animals. In fact, no one had told me what to think about anything. I saw what I saw and made what I made of it.

Once I got myself into the proper "stranded on a desert island" mindset, I picked up the Bible and read the red parts. By the time I was finished reading, I was feeling rather astonished. I couldn't fathom at all how the modern Christian world had sprung from Christ's words. It was quite an eye-opener.

So, when confusion threatened to overwhelm me as I began to read the other sacred scripture, I drew upon this previous experience. Stranding myself on the desert island, I would pick up a holy book with the same curiosity of finding a beautiful exotic shell on the beach. One day it would be the Koran. The next, it would be the Torah. The day after that, the Bhagavad Gita. I would regard the book with curiosity: "Hmmm, what's this? I've never heard of *this* before."

And then I would open it and read. I read without fear or prejudice. I read only with a curious and open mind, as I would study any new phenomenon heretofore unseen. I came upon things that puzzled me. I came upon things that made no sense at all to me. And I came upon things that I *did* understand and could easily relate to.

One thing I like about my desert island exercise is that it honestly reflects my condition. I do live on a desert island, of sorts, in the sense that I am isolated from the cultures to which these scriptures were delivered. I have little understanding of the ins and outs of daily life for people who lived so many centuries—even millennia—ago. I do not really know how people in those places and times saw the world or regarded their place in it. How can I, when I am so permeated with the values and concepts of the twenty-first century? While I can read history and learn something about these cultures, I cannot experience life the way the people living back then experienced it, and can only view those time periods as an outsider.

In addition to the culture gap, these scriptures also represent a time gap. Cultures are not static; they tend to develop. Things change. A Jew today lives in a very different world from a Jew in the days of Moses. A Christian today lives in a very different world than that of Christ's day. The same can be said for Zoroastrians, Buddhists, Hindus, and Muslims. Dramatic changes have swept over the entire planet in the past century alone. Our paradigms are different from those of our forbears, as are our technologies and many of our problems. Our limitations, capabilities, and opportunities little resemble those of our distant ancestors.

Such a gulf exists between me and those distant peoples, direct ancestors or not, that no matter the line of my descent, I am, indeed, stranded on a desert island from them. Even those scriptures that are a formative component of the culture of my ancestors, and which may still color aspects of my own culture, may no longer make much sense to me.

But here and there I do find myself in recognizable territory. I understand the subject being addressed. And the interesting thing is, it's always about the same subject. As Bahá'u'lláh said, the Manifestations of God *do* share a common mission. Whether it's Moses, Muḥammad, Buddha, or Jesus, the content is extraordinarily consistent. You won't be surprised by now, I hope, when I tell you that it always addresses our virtuous qualities.

Here is a sampling:

Krishna:
Humbleness, truthfulness, and harmlessness,
Patience and honour, reverence for the wise,

Purity, constancy, control of self,
Contempt of self-delights, self-sacrifice,
Perception of the certitude of ill
In birth, death, age, disease, suffering, and sin;
Detachment, lightly holding unto home,
Children, and wife, and all that bindeth men;
An ever-tranquil heart in fortunes good
And fortunes evil, with a will set firm
To worship Me—Me only! ceasing not;
Loving all solitudes, and shunning noise
Of foolish crowds; endeavor resolute
To reach perception of the Utmost Soul,
And grace to understand what gain it were
So to attain,—this is true Wisdom, Prince!
And what is otherwise is ignorance![3]

Moses:

The Lord spoke to Moses, saying: Speak to the whole Israelite community and say to them:

You shall be holy, for I, the Lord your God, am holy.

You shall each revere his mother and his father, and keep My Sabbaths: I the Lord am your God. . . .

When you reap the harvest of your land, you shall not reap all the way to the edges of your field, or gather the gleanings of your harvest. You shall not pick your vineyard bare, or gather the fallen fruit of your vineyard; you shall leave them for the poor and the stranger: I the Lord am your God.

You shall not steal; you shall not deal deceitfully or falsely with one another. You shall not swear falsely by My name, profaning the name of your God: I am the Lord.

You shall not defraud your fellow. You shall not commit robbery. The wages of a laborer shall not remain with you until morning.

You shall not insult the deaf, or place a stumbling block before the blind. You shall fear your God: I am the Lord.

You shall not render an unfair decision: do not favor the poor or show deference to the rich; judge your kinsman fairly. Do not deal basely with your countrymen. Do not profit by the blood of your fellow: I am the Lord.

You shall not hate your kinsfolk in your heart. Reprove your kinsman but incur no guilt because of him. You shall not take vengeance or bear a grudge against your countrymen. Love your fellow as yourself: I am the Lord. . . .

When a stranger resides with you in your land, you shall not wrong him. The stranger who resides with you shall be to you as one of your citizens; you shall love him as yourself, for you were strangers in the land of Egypt: I the Lord am your God.

You shall not falsify measures of length, weight, or capacity. . . .

I the Lord am your God who freed you from the land of Egypt. You shall faithfully observe all My laws and rules: I am the Lord.[4]

Zoroaster:
Let man toil with his thought and the actions of both hands
to frustrate
the Followers of the Lie.
Let him lead his fellowmen towards the good.
He is then in harmony with the Will of Ahura*
and rejoices Mazda.
A member of the family, the community or the clan
should do his best for the righteous.
He must nourish the living with zeal.
He will then dwell
in lush pastures of Truth and the Good Mind,
O Ahura.
So I will pray away disobedience and evil thought
from You, O Mazda,
perversity from the family,
insidious deceit from the community,
slanderers from the clan,
and from life's pastures the most darkened mind.
I will now invoke for You and for the Final Goal
the most mighty Sraosha (willing obedience to Mazda).
Only then can I gain

* Ahura Mazda—"Lord of Life," the Zoroastrian name for God.

the long-lasting Sovereignty of the Good Mind
along the straight paths of Truth
Where You, O Ahura Mazda, dwell.[5]

Gautama Buddha:
This is what should be done by the man who is wise, who seeks the good, and who knows the meaning of the place of peace.

Let him be strenuous, upright, and truly straight, without conceit of self, easily contented and joyous, free of cares; let him not be submerged by the things of the world; let him not take upon himself the burden of worldly goods; let his senses be controlled; let him be wise but not puffed up, and let him not desire great possessions even for his family. Let him do nothing that is mean or that the wise would reprove.

May all beings be happy and at their ease! May they be joyous and live in safety!

All beings, whether weak or strong—omitting none—in high, middle, or low realms of existence, small or great, visible or invisible, near or far away, born or to be born—may all beings be happy and at their ease!

Let none deceive another, or despise any being in any state! Let none by anger or ill-will wish harm to another!

Even as a mother watches over and protects her child, her only child, so with a boundless mind should one cherish all living beings, radiating friendliness over the entire world, above, below, and all around without limit. So let him cultivate a boundless good will towards the entire world, uncramped, free from ill-will or enmity.

Standing or walking, sitting or lying down, during all his waking hours, let him establish this mindfulness of good will, which men call the highest state!

Abandoning vain discussions, having a clear vision, free from sense appetites, he who is made perfect will never again know rebirth.[6]

Jesus Christ:
But I say unto you which hear, Love your enemies, do good to them which hate you,

Bless them that curse you, and pray for them which despitefully use you.

And unto him that smiteth thee on the one cheek offer also the other; and him that taketh away thy cloke forbid not to take thy coat also.

Give to every man that asketh of thee; and of him that taketh away thy goods ask them not again.

And as you would that men should do to you, do ye also to them likewise.

For if you love them which love you, what thank have ye? for sinners also love those that love them.

And if ye do good to them which do good to you, what thank have ye? for sinners also do even the same.

And if ye lend to them of whom ye hope to receive, what thank have ye? for sinners also lend to sinners, to receive as much again.

But love ye your enemies, and do good, and lend, hoping for nothing again; and your reward shall be great, and ye shall be the children of the Highest: for he is kind unto the unthankful and to the evil.

Be ye therefore merciful, as your Father also is merciful.

Judge not, and ye shall not be judged: condemn not, and ye shall not be condemned: forgive, and ye shall be forgiven:

Give, and it shall be given unto you; good measure, pressed down, and shaken together, and running over, shall men give into your bosom. For with the same measure that ye mete withal it shall be measured to you again.[7]

Muḥammad:

Worship God, and join not aught with Him in worship. Be good to parents, and to kindred, and to orphans, and to the poor, and to a neighbour, whether kinsman or new-comer, and to a fellow traveller, and to the wayfarer, and to the slaves whom your right hands hold; verily, God loveth not the proud, the vain boaster,

Who are niggardly themselves, and bid others to be niggards, and hide away what God of his bounty hath given them. We have made ready a shameful chastisement for the unbelievers,

And for those who bestow their substance in alms to be seen of men, and believe not in God and in the last day. Whoever hath Satan for his companion, an evil companion has he!

But what blessedness would be theirs, if they should believe in God and in the last day, and bestow alms out of what God hath vouchsafed them; for God taketh knowledge of them!

God truly will not wrong any one of the weight of a mote; and if there be any good deed, he will repay it doubly; and from his presence shall be given a great recompense.[8]

Bahá'u'lláh:
Be generous in prosperity, and thankful in adversity. Be worthy of the trust
of thy neighbor, and look upon him with a bright and friendly face. Be a
treasure to the poor, an admonisher to the rich, an answerer of the cry of the
needy, a preserver of the sanctity of thy pledge. Be fair in thy judgment, and
guarded in thy speech. Be unjust to no man, and show all meekness to all
men. Be as a lamp unto them that walk in darkness, a joy to the sorrowful,
a sea for the thirsty, a haven for the distressed, an upholder and defender
of the victim of oppression. Let integrity and uprightness distinguish all
thine acts. Be a home for the stranger, a balm to the suffering, a tower of
strength for the fugitive. Be eyes to the blind, and a guiding light unto the
feet of the erring. Be an ornament to the countenance of truth, a crown to
the brow of fidelity, a pillar of the temple of righteousness, a breath of life
to the body of mankind, an ensign of the hosts of justice, a luminary above
the horizon of virtue, a dew to the soil of the human heart, an ark on the
ocean of knowledge, a sun in the heaven of bounty, a gem on the diadem
of wisdom, a shining light in the firmament of thy generation, a fruit upon
the tree of humility.[9]

Unlike those sacred writings that deal with laws and ordinances, these examples show an aspect of scripture that is timeless and universal in nature. They set
forth principles that can be understood by all people, in all cultures, and at every
point in history. These are directives that transcend cultural values and speak to
the heart—the very nature—of every human being. These passages identify the
virtuous qualities latent within us and instruct us on how to cultivate and express
them. This theme of cultivating virtuous qualities forms the core of each holy
book, and it remains absolutely consistent, no matter the cultural context, from
one Manifestation of God to the next.

In these scriptures, virtuous ideals, qualities, and conditions are clearly laid
out for us and give life, vigor, and expression to otherwise vague impulses that
might very well be overridden by cultural pressures or our more basic emotional
and physical drives. As we learn about our virtuous qualities and practice them,
we become less interested in putting ourselves first and become more interested
in putting others first. Throughout history, humanity has been educated by these
instructions, and through them, we can realize the fullness of our human potential. With this in mind, let's spend a little time exploring the content of these
quoted scriptures.

The True Measure of Success

Knowledge in action emerges as the objective of virtuous development. In its simplest form, knowledge in action can be expressed in two words: "Do good." With these two words, we are challenged in both thought and deed, for this is a call to right action. First we must understand what is good (which requires knowledge), and then we must find a way to express it (which requires action).

So, what is "good"? Is what I want good? Is getting my own way good? Is having enough food to eat good? Is wealth good? Is power good? Is obedience to those in authority good?

Left to our own devices, we often tend to operate as if all these things are good. After all, much of what we do is centered exactly on those things. How much thought and activity goes into getting our own way, acquiring power, accumulating wealth, or following the boss's orders? No doubt, a good deal.

But the Manifestations of God step in and tell us that humility, truthfulness, and patience are good. We learn that truth is good, that loving the stranger is good, and that cherishing all that exists is good. We learn that generosity is good and that being a balm to others who are suffering is good.

While our culture may tell us that wealth, power, status, marriage, or children are measures of success, the Manifestations of God bring us a very different way of viewing success. Not once do They tell us to seek material riches; instead, They tell us to be generous. Never do They tell us to do whatever it takes to get our own way. Instead, They tell us to serve others and to be honest and trustworthy. Never do they promote blind obedience to those in power. Instead, They tell us to defend the oppressed, to love our enemies, and to worship only God. In fact, success, by Their definition and example, is to be measured by how well we cultivate and express our virtuous powers.

Success: What to do

According to the Bhagavad Gita, success looks like this: as far as others are concerned, we are to revere the wise, be humble, truthful, patient, and honorable. As far as the self is concerned, we are to be pure, constant, exercise self-control, and be willing to sacrifice.

To discover the true meaning of these qualities and then to express them in action is a challenge of Herculean proportions. Thus, with just a few words, the Manifestations of God set us on a path like no other, for it is a path of unparalleled depth and breadth. Our old measure of success crumbles to dust to be replaced by a measure of incomparable worth.

Zoroaster instructs His followers to toil with "thought and action of both hands to frustrate the followers of the Lie" in order, ultimately, to lead others toward the good. This statement highlights the balance between knowledge and action, for without knowledge of the truth and what is good, one cannot expose falsehood (the "Lie"). Without action, one cannot lead others to the good.

Buddha offers a long list to those wise ones who seek the good. For starters, one should be strenuous, upright, truly straight, and without self-conceit. He further tells us that with a "boundless mind," we should "cherish all living beings . . . above, below, and all around without limit." During all our waking hours, throughout all our activities, we are to establish a mindfulness of goodwill toward the entire world. The story of the Buddha's life is a demonstration of these principles.

Christ offers some very specific examples of what this new measure of success can look like in action: if someone takes your cloak, you must also let him have your coat; if someone curses you and despitefully uses you, you must pray for him; if someone hates you, you are to do good for him. Surely, to return love for hate and good deeds for misdeeds is the acme of human behavior, a true flowering of human potential.

Muḥammad instructs us to be good to anyone who might cross our path, no matter their station: parents, kindred, orphans, the poor, neighbors, newcomers, fellow travelers, the wayfarer, even slaves. He admonishes us to guard against pride and boasting. He prohibits being stingy, hoarding wealth, showing it off, or using it to impress others. According to Muḥammad, we should measure success not by accumulating wealth but by sharing it. And even then, it must be shared in a way that doesn't cultivate pride or self-promotion.

In the passage from Bahá'u'lláh, we find many examples of this new measure of success. We are to be generous in prosperity, a treasure to the poor, an admonisher to the rich, a preserver of our pledge, fair in our judgment, guarded in our speech, unjust to no one, meek to all, a balm to the suffering, and a tower of strength for the fugitive.

Success: What not to do

The Manifestations of God not only tell us what to do, They also often tell us what *not* to do. Many of the laws of Moses are prohibitions, such as to refrain from dealing deceitfully with our neighbors, to not render an unfair decision, and to not take vengeance or bear a grudge. If we turn these "don'ts" into "dos," we actually end up with a list of virtues. With all those don'ts, Moses is essentially telling His followers to be honest, just, and forgiving. But in this case, we achieve our goal by *refraining* from certain kinds of conduct.

Krishna tells us to shun the noise of foolish crowds. The "do" here is to seek silence and / or wise company. Zoroaster declares that He will pray away disobedience and evil thought. The "do" here is obedience and good thought. Buddha tells us not to be puffed up, not to desire great possessions, and not to deceive or despise anyone. In other words, we should be humble, live simply, and be honest and loving. Jesus tells us not to judge or condemn. The "do" here is to accept and forgive. Muḥammad warns us that God does not love the proud, the boaster, or the niggardly. In other words, we should strive to be humble, observe silence, and be generous. Bahá'u'lláh warns us away from unjustness. The "do" here is to be just.

The power behind these prohibitions is that by not doing that which might come naturally or most easily, or that which strong emotions, passion, or self-interest move us to do, we take a step toward doing good. When we don't deal deceitfully, we take a step toward becoming honest. When we don't render an unfair decision, we take a step toward becoming just. When we don't take vengeance or bear a grudge, we take a step toward forgiveness.

Remember, the goal here is virtuous development. It isn't always enough to be told to "be nice" or what to do. We sometimes have to hear "stop," or what not to do. Prohibitions serve to arrest destructive, inappropriate, or nonproductive behavior and force us to seek an alternate path that will lead toward virtuous development.

Finding True Love

What we are learning to do during this phase of development is, as Moses put it, to "Love your fellow as yourself." Or, as Buddha stated, we are learning to "cultivate a boundless good will toward the entire world, uncramped, free from ill-will or enmity." During this stage of development, we learn to become ardent lovers of humanity. The Manifestations of God speak quite plainly about this love.

This is a love that might be described as altruistic. I find Buddha's description of this love compelling: "Even as a mother watches over and protects her child, her only child, so with a boundless mind should one cherish all living beings . . . above, below, and all around without limit."

Think about that statement. Think about the difference between a mother and a child. A child is at the mercy of the mother, just as a weak person is at the mercy of a strong person or a poor person is at the mercy of a rich person. A good mother does not neglect her child, nor does she take advantage of her superior position in order to manipulate or use the child to her own advantage. To do so is the antithesis of love and a violation of the role of motherhood. A good mother puts the child's welfare before her own, uses her superior position to watch over and protect her child, and ensures that her child has the opportunity to achieve his or her greatest potential. Buddha essentially asks us to watch over and protect every other thing with that same attitude.

The love we are cultivating is not to be directed only toward those we like or toward those for whom we hold affection and regard. Nor is it reserved for the strong and powerful or for those from whom we may expect recompense or gain. This love is universal and all-encompassing, and it must include the weakest among us and even those we like the least.

In fact, the Manifestations of God are quite clear about how we should treat those who may wish us ill, or those who are weaker, poorer, or less educated than we are, or otherwise at a disadvantage.

Moses exhorts us not to victimize the disadvantaged: "You shall not defraud your fellow . . . commit robbery . . . insult the deaf, or place a stumbling block before the blind." And Christ exhorts us to "Love your enemies, and do good, and lend, hoping for nothing again." Muḥammad tells us to be good to the poor, to orphans and slaves, and to pay alms.

Bahá'u'lláh, too, charges the strong with care of the weak: "Be eyes to the blind, and a guiding light unto the feet of the erring." I find it interesting that Bahá'u'lláh refers to blindness, as did Moses. In this context, however, it becomes clear that blindness can be a metaphor for ignorance or the blind faith through which people cling to false beliefs.

Suddenly, Moses' warnings not to insult the deaf or place a stumbling block before the blind—an admonition I had considered odd (I had to wonder, were people really that hurtful back then?)—makes new sense to me when I realize they were actually referring to one's spiritual state. I make a connection back to the beginning of Christ's sermon in which He says His message is for those who will hear. I realize that blindness and deafness can be metaphors for spiritual blindness and deafness, or ignorance, gullibility, and even obstinacy. These kinds of blindness and deafness are more serious than the physical kind. Yet we are told to treat all forms of blindness and deafness, indeed all forms of weakness, in the same way. Do not abuse, insult, or take advantage of them, Moses warns. Protect and guide them, Bahá'u'lláh directs.

The love we are told to cultivate is also to be extended to strangers. Moses tells us to love the stranger as we love ourselves. Muḥammad tells us to be good to the newcomer, the fellow traveler, and the wayfarer.

Bahá'u'lláh tells us to be a home for the stranger. In my dictionary, I found many definitions for the word *home*, but the one that I think fits is "an environment or haven of shelter, happiness and love." While I had expected the "shelter" part of the definition, the part about a home being a place of happiness and love took me by surprise. And I noticed that Bahá'u'lláh did not say to provide shelter; instead, He said to *be* a haven of shelter, happiness, and love to the stranger. Was He telling me that I needed to remake myself so that even a stranger would feel sheltered, happy, and loved in my presence and that others would be able to find in me the same security they experience in their own homes?

I must ask myself: how long will it take before all this becomes second nature to me, as effortless as reading is to me now? I am not sure it will *ever* become second nature to me; still, the standard has been set, the challenge presented, and I cannot turn my back on it.

Our actions and responsibilities are not confined to the examples mentioned in sacred scripture. The Manifestations of God cannot cover every possible contingency, and I am convinced They would not try, in any case. To list every possibility would reduce us to being simple rule-followers. Deprived of the opportunity for struggle and the learning that results from it, our concern would be for the letter of the law and not for the spirit.

Using the examples and words of the Manifestations of God, we must face the inevitable truth that our focus and concern must ripple out into every aspect of life and that our strengths and advantages must be put to the service of those who are weak and disadvantaged. Thus the seeing must be eyes to the blind. Those in power must use their influence to help the downtrodden and oppressed. The wealthy must aid and succor the poor. The wise must guide the foolish. The educated must assist the ignorant. Throughout the world, men—who generally enjoy advantages over women due solely to gender—must champion equal rights and opportunities for women.

Whatever our advantages may be in this life—be it gender, race, wealth, power, status, intelligence, education—they do not give us the right to exploit others, but rather the responsibility to help those in need. At every moment, we are called upon to use these advantages and these strengths to be of service to those without them.

To take on such a virtuous objective is exceedingly difficult, and it can stand in the way of achieving more immediate gratification. How can I obtain a fine home and accumulate wealth if I am generous with the poor? How can I get ahead in business or politics if I am kind to my enemies?

Often we rationalize our way around these things and decide that, in order to accomplish something for the larger good, we must make a few moral compromises along the way. Perhaps we will conclude that the poor just haven't worked hard enough or that our rivals are not good people and deserve to be penalized. We have many ways of doing exactly what we want without feeling too guilty about it.

Our desires are most often and naturally turned toward the things of this human and material world. We may desire possessions, power, or the admiration of others. We are easily diverted, desiring to distraction one day and then losing interest the next. Instead of striving for virtuous success, we bend all our thoughts and energies toward satisfying our worldly cravings and promoting our own interests. In doing so, we sacrifice our virtuous development.

This is not just a bad trade-off. It's the worst swap possible, the mistake of a lifetime.

As I perused sacred scriptures, I found that another common thread ran through them all. Along with the universal counsel that directs us to right action, I discovered a universal promise of a reward if we do good and a universal warning of dire consequences if we don't. As you will see in the next chapter, ignoring the directives of the Manifestations of God puts us in great peril, and what we do or don't do today has far-reaching consequences for the future.

13

Reward and Punishment

As I was searching through scripture for references to virtuous development, I couldn't avoid the discovery of another topic that had universal coverage. I made note of it as I went along but put it aside, unsure what to do about it. The subject made me decidedly uncomfortable. It brought back all the anxieties I had experienced as a child learning the Catholic catechism with its what I call "if you can't talk them into it, scare them into it" approach: the threat of punishment—eternal, horrible, and inescapable—if you rejected the Church's interpretation of scripture.

This was a topic I had come to resent, for I had been terrorized with the threat since childhood. I also see many Christian denominations that, while they are eager to distance themselves from the Catholic Church, are not shy about using the same "scare them into it" approach to teaching. I've seen many TV preachers praising God one moment and in the next damning the unsaved / infidel / sinner to hell. Once I even attended a church whose pastor praised its members (the *real* saved people) while disparaging the Christian congregation down the street, who weren't really saved. *They* aren't actually the saved ones; *we* are. And so it goes, that message that *we have it right, and you are not only wrong but will be eternally punished,* that some people proclaim so loudly.

Despite my discomfort, I finally realized that, since this is a common theme, I needed to face my fears and personal prejudice against the topic and take an open-minded look at it. I'm glad I did. It's not at all the club that the self-righteous seem to brandish with glee.

What I discovered is that, while people tend to threaten you with eternal punishment for not believing what they want you to believe, scripture actually refers to punishment as a consequence for rejecting truth and failing to take right action.

131

It is important to get a grasp of the topic, for much is at stake. So, without fear or prejudice, let's take a look at how reward and punishment is addressed in scripture.

Krishna:
Moreover, when a soul departeth, fixed
In Soothfastness,* it goeth to the place—
Perfect and pure—of those that know all Truth.
If it departeth in set habitude
Of Impulse, it shall pass into the world
Of spirits tied to works; and if it dies
In hardened Ignorance, that blinded soul
Is born anew in some unlighted womb.

The fruit of Soothfastness is true and sweet;
The fruit of lusts is pain and toil; the fruit
Of Ignorance is deeper darkness. Yea!
For Light brings light; and Passion ache to have;
And gloom, bewilderments, and ignorance
Grow forth from Ignorance. Those of the first
Rise ever higher; those of the second mode
Take a mid place; the darkened souls sink back
To lower deeps, loaded with witlessness![1]

Moses:
See, I set before you this day life and prosperity, death and adversity. For I command you this day, to love the Lord your God, to walk in His ways, and to keep His commandments, His laws, and His rules, that you may thrive and increase, and that the Lord your God may bless you in the land that you are about to enter and possess. But if your heart turns away and you give no heed, and are lured into the worship and service of other gods, I declare to you this day that you shall certainly perish; you shall not long endure on the soil that you are crossing the Jordan to enter and possess. I call heaven and earth to witness against you this day: I have put before you life and death, blessing and curse. Choose life—if you and your offspring would

---

* Truth.

live—by loving the Lord your God, heeding his commands, and holding fast to Him. For thereby you shall have life and shall long endure upon the soil that the Lord swore to your ancestors . . .[2]

Zoroaster:
Whoever clings to the Followers of Truth,
his dwelling shall be the Light.
But for you,
O Worshippers of Falsehood,
a long life of darkness, foul food and woeful wailings—
to such an existence
will your evil conscience
lead you through your own deeds.

But to him who is His friend
in thought and act
Ahura Mazda will grant
Perfection and Immortality,
and out of His Abundance Truth,
His Sovereignty and the firm support
of the Good Mind.[3]

Gautama Buddha:
The evil-doer grieves in this world, he grieves in the next, he grieves in both. He grieves, he is afflicted, seeing the evil of his own actions.

The righteous man rejoices in the world, he rejoices in the next; he rejoices in both. He rejoices and becomes delighted seeing the purity of his actions.

The evil-doer suffers in this world, he suffers in the next; he suffers in both. He suffers (thinking) "evil has been done by me." He suffers even more when he has gone to the evil place. The righteous man rejoices in this world, he rejoices in the next; he rejoices in both. He rejoices (thinking) "good has been done by me." He rejoices still more when he has gone to the good place.[4]

Jesus Christ:
When the son of man shall come in his glory, and all the holy angels with him, then shall he sit upon the throne of his glory:

And before him shall be gathered all nations: and he shall separate them one from another, as a shepherd divideth his sheep from the goats:

And he shall set the sheep on his right hand, but the goats on the left.

Then shall the King say unto them on his right hand, Come, ye blessed of my Father, inherit the kingdom prepared for you from the foundation of the world:

For I was an hungred and ye gave me meat: I was thirsty, and ye gave me drink: I was a stranger and ye took me in:

Naked, and ye clothed me: I was sick, and ye visited me: I was in prison, and ye came unto me.

Then shall the righteous answer him, saying, Lord, when saw we thee an hungred, and fed thee? Or thirsty, and gave thee drink?

When saw we thee a stranger, and took thee in? or naked, and clothed thee?

Or when saw we thee sick, or in prison, and came unto thee?

And the King shall answer and say unto them, Verily I say unto you, Inasmuch as ye have done it unto one of the least of these my brethren, ye have done it unto me.

Then shall he say also unto them on the left hand, Depart from me, ye cursed, into everlasting fire, prepared for the devil and his angels:

For I was an hungred, and ye gave me no meat: I was thirsty, and ye gave me no drink:

I was a stranger and ye took me not in: naked, and ye clothed me not: sick, and in prison, and ye visited me not.

Then shall they also answer him, saying, Lord, when saw we thee an hungred, or athirst, or a stranger, or naked, or sick, or in prison, and did not minister unto thee?

Then shall he answer them, saying, Verily I say unto you, Inasmuch as ye did it not to one of the least of these, ye did it not to me.

And these shall go away into everlasting punishment: but the righteous into life eternal.[5]

Muḥammad:
By the night when she spreads her veil;
By the Day when it brightly shineth;
By Him who made male and female;
At different ends truly do ye aim!
But as to him who giveth alms and feareth God,

And yieldeth assent to the Good;
To him will we make easy the path to happiness.
But as to him who is covetous and bent on riches,
And calleth the Good a lie,
To him will we make easy the path to misery:
And what shall his wealth avail him when he goeth down?
Truly man's guidance is with Us
And Ours, the Future and the Past.
I warn you therefore of the flaming fire;
None shall be cast to it but the most wretched,—
Who hath called the truth a lie and turned his back.
But the God-fearing shall escape it,—
Who giveth away his substance that he may become pure;
And who offereth not favours to any one for the sake of recompense,
But only as seeking the face of his Lord the Most High.
And surely in the end he shall be well content.[6]

Bahá'u'lláh:

And now concerning thy question whether human souls continue to be conscious one of another after their separation from the body. . . . The people of Bahá*, who are the inmates of the Ark of God, are, one and all, well aware of one another's state and condition, and are united in the bonds of intimacy and fellowship. Such a state, however, must depend upon their faith and their conduct. They that are of the same grade and station are fully aware of one another's capacity, character, accomplishments and merits. They that are of a lower grade, however, are incapable of comprehending adequately the station, or of estimating the merits, of those that rank above them. Each shall receive his share from thy Lord. Blessed is the man that hath turned his face towards God, and walked steadfastly in His love, until his soul hath winged its flight unto God, the Sovereign Lord of all, the Most Powerful, the Ever-Forgiving, the All-Merciful.

The souls of the infidels, however, shall—and to this I bear witness—when breathing their last be made aware of the good things that have

---

* Those who believe in Bahá'u'lláh and obey His teachings.

135

escaped them, and shall bemoan their plight, and shall humble themselves before God. They shall continue doing so after the separation of their souls from their bodies.

It is clear and evident that all men shall, after their physical death, estimate the worth of their deeds, and realize all that their hands have wrought. I swear by the Daystar that shineth above the horizon of Divine power! They that are the followers of the one true God shall, the moment they depart out of this life, experience such joy and gladness as would be impossible to describe, while they that live in error shall be seized with such fear and trembling, and shall be filled with such consternation, as nothing can exceed. Well is it with him that hath quaffed the choice and incorruptible wine of faith through the gracious favor and the manifold bounties of Him Who is the Lord of all Faiths.[7]

This is a lot to take in, I know. I confess that while I was analyzing these texts, my mind would go into a fog. But I was determined to get a grip on the subject of reward and punishment and really comprehend it. Perseverance paid off. Finally, I recognized the common components, and when I organized the scriptures into charts, the information became not only manageable, but intriguing.

These charts crystallize the universality of the themes of reward and punishment. These are pretty simple charts, really, and they analyze the passages of scripture into four categories: Who Gets Rewarded, The Reward, Who Gets Punished, and The Punishment. Not only is it easy to follow, but some commonalities immediately emerge.

On the one hand, we have those who are rewarded: those who are fixed in soothfastness (that is, truth), are the followers of the one true God, and are obedient to His commandments; those who do good; and the righteous. In fact, each scripture promises reward for the same kind of person. This is a description of a good person, whose focus is on truth and reality, and who is dedicated to the process of virtuous development.

On the other hand, we have those who are punished: the soul hardened in ignorance, the soul that is impulsive, the worshipper of falsehood, those who worship other gods, the evil-doers, those who disobey God's command, the unrighteous, those who call the good a lie, and those who live in error. Here we find the descriptions of two kinds of people—someone who could be called evil, and someone who is not necessarily evil but not virtuous, either. Basically, "living in error" describes both kinds of people.

Manifestation of God	Who Gets Rewarded	The Reward
Krishna (Bhagavad Gita)	A soul fixed in Soothfast-ness (truth).	Going to the place, perfect and pure, of those that know all Truth; fruits are true and sweet; soul will rise higher; light brings light.
Moses (Torah)	Those who keep God's commandments.	Life and prosperity; will thrive and increase; shall have life and long endure upon the soil the Lord swore to your ancestors.
Zoroaster (Gathas)	Whoever clings to the Fol-lowers of Truth; the friend of Ahura Mazda in thought and act.	Dwelling shall be light; perfection and immortality.
Buddha (Dhammapada)	The righteous man.	Rejoices in this world and in the next, becomes delighted seeing the purity of his ac-tions; he rejoices (thinking) "good has been done by me." Rejoices more when he goes to the good place.
Jesus Christ (Matthew)	The righteous.	Inherit the kingdom prepared for you from the foundation of the world; eternal life.
Muḥammad (Sura 92)	Those who give alms and fear God, and yield assent to the good.	Make easy the path to happiness; shall be well content.
Bahá'u'lláh (Gleanings, no. 86.2)	Followers of the one true God.	Those who are the inmates of the Ark of God are well aware of one another's state and condition; united in the bond of intimacy and fellowship; experience such joy and gladness, impos-sible to describe.

Manifestation of God	Who Gets Punished	The Punishment
Krishna (Bhagavad Gita)	A soul in set habitude of impulse.	If it departs in set habitude of impulse, it passes into the world of spirits tied to works; the fruit of lusts is pain and toil.
	A soul hardened in ignorance.	(Takes a mid place); if it dies in hardened ignorance, it is born anew in some un-lighted womb; gloom, bewilderment, and ignorance come from ignorance; the fruit of ignorance is deeper darkness.
	Darkened souls.	Darkened souls sink back to lower deeps, loaded with witlessness.
Moses (Torah)	Those who turn away, and are lured into the worship and service of other gods.	Death and adversity; you shall certainly perish, and not long endure upon the soil.
Zoroaster (Gathas)	Worshippers of Falsehood.	Long life of darkness, foul food, and woeful wailing. Evil conscience leads you through your own deeds.
Buddha (Dhammapada)	The evil-doer.	Grieves in this world and in the next, afflicted seeing the evil of his actions; suffers in this world and in the next, (thinking) "evil has been done by me." Suffers even more when he goes to the evil place.
Jesus Christ (Matthew)	The unrighteous.	Depart into everlasting fire; everlasting punishment.
Muḥammad (Sura 92)	Him who is covetous and bent of riches, and called the good a lie.	Make easy the path to misery; none but the most wretched cast into flaming fire.
Bahá'u'lláh (Gleanings, no. 86.2)	They that live in error.	They that are of a lower grade incapable of comprehending the station or estimating the merits of those that rank above them; souls of infidels will be made aware of the good things that have escaped them, shall bemoan their plight, and shall humble themselves before God; shall be seized with such fear and trembling, shall be filled with such consternation, as nothing can exceed.

These descriptions bring to mind the parable of the Good Samaritan discussed in chapter 8. On one end of the spectrum we have the Samaritan, who goes well out of his way to succor a stranger. On the other end of the spectrum we have the robbers, who beat the traveler almost to death in order to acquire his property for themselves.

The priest and the Levite fall into the middle, and they represent the majority of us. They have come to live in error by placing the purity laws or their own welfare above the welfare of another. One can certainly fall into error by becoming overly concerned with adherence to the letter of the law, thereby sacrificing the very spiritual development the laws were designed to protect. It is a condition that Christ warned his contemporaries against.

The priest and the Levite conformed to the law that should have made them right with God, and they enjoyed the populace's good opinion. But when it came down to it, they were not prepared to do the right thing. Of what good is adherence to the law if one remains a stranger to kindness, love, compassion, and selflessness?

Since I have already spoken at length about virtuousness, let's focus awhile on what happens when we don't pursue that path. According to the list, the alternative is to become one who lives in error, is impulsive, hardened in ignorance, who worships falsehood and false gods, who is darkened, unrighteous, or does evil.

While virtuous development takes conscious effort, following one's impulses is simply the path of least resistance. It is the path of no virtuous effort. Really, we are born impulsive, and to remain motivated by our every desire is to remain in a childlike condition. An impulsive person avoids self-examination, justifies his motives instead of questioning them, and is not acquainted very well with his spiritual nature. Instead, he is most acquainted with his current appetites.

An impulsive person's motivation is the satisfaction of those appetites. When a person is impulsive, he cannot be obedient to God. Instead, he obeys the demands of his own appetites and desires. This is a restless path, as appetites can only be temporarily satisfied. It is a path that brings neither rest nor peace.

An ignorant person is without the means to discriminate between truth and falsehood and is thus easily manipulated, easily turned from the critical process of virtuous development. In this condition, we find no shortage of false gods to worship. A false god, in this context, is whatever drives you or informs your life that is not actually God. Perhaps it is the attainment of wealth or power or adhering to racial, cultural, religious, or national ideologies. Perhaps it is the drive to be successful in business or to be the top person in your field. Perhaps you consider all of your opinions correct and, by thus granting yourself infallibility, become your own false god.

The impulsive or ignorant person is unmindful of spiritual qualities or his own spiritual nature. He therefore lacks the most essential knowledge—the knowledge of self. To avoid the slide into evil, it is important to acquire self-knowledge and become aware of your motives, strengths, weaknesses, and limitations. It is important to become acquainted with that part of yourself that is not physical or attached to appetites.

Above all things, self-knowledge requires truthfulness, for the path of virtuous development requires honest self-examination. Vigilance is called for as we try to determine how we failed to act virtuously, how to do better the next time, what virtues are being called for, and how to apply them to a situation.

The worshipper of falsehood, the unrighteous, and those who call the good a lie are pretty much the same kind of people. I can think of some major historical figures, power-hungry tyrants, who fit into this category. Adolf Hitler certainly worshipped falsehood when he promoted the superiority of the Aryan race. And he alone is not to blame for the devastation and death meted out to countless innocents during his reign. His name would never have been known had it not been for the innumerable and mostly nameless other worshippers of falsehood who carried out his malign ambitions in ways both large and small.

Most of us don't go around thinking, "Oh goody, I think I'll go do some evil." Instead, we bury our motives beneath a veneer of righteousness, or a complex, self-deceptive web of rationalization.

Someone who steals may decide that she needs the desired item more than its owner does. Perhaps someone justifies an angry rebuke to his neighbor for not following the "one true religion"—which is his own, obviously—under the pretense of trying to save his neighbor's soul. Or someone may manipulate or pressure others into doing something they would prefer not to, rationalizing it as necessary "for their own good." A parent who strikes a stubborn child will claim "he asked for it," and call her own angry outburst an act of discipline. An accountant who doctors the books to make a company look profitable will simply claim he is obeying his boss. Or a salesman who lies about the quality of a product to make a sale will call the buyer a fool who deserves what she gets.

No one is exempt from temptations and pressures. We are all daily witnesses to them or are involved in them. If someone cuts me off in traffic, do I respond in delightfully cathartic anger? If I am mistreated by someone, do I justify revenge? Do I engage in the fun of spreading rumors and gossip? Do I backbite the folks I don't like? Do I "constructively" criticize the people around me? Do I feel entitled to do or have whatever I want, despite the impact on others?

If we can't virtuously direct our behavior over everyday situations, then what do we do when something larger looms? If we rationalize or blame others for our bad actions, it is a sure sign that we are on the wrong path, a path that will only lead to great regret and unhappiness.

The Punishment

I find in the scriptures two aspects of punishment. One is that we become conscious of the evil we have done. Zoroaster warns that "to such an existence will your evil conscience lead you through your own deeds." Buddha warns that "the evil doer suffers (thinking) 'evil has been done by me' even more when he has gone to the evil place." Bahá'u'lláh also warns that "men shall, after their physical death, estimate the worth of their deeds, and realize all that their hands have wrought. . . . They that live in error shall be seized with such fear and trembling, and shall be filled with such consternation, as nothing can exceed."

This describes a type of awakening, becoming undeniably aware of our deeds, that which our "hands have wrought." In this condition we can no longer rationalize, no longer deceive ourselves. Every form of self-deception is stripped away, and we see our actions in the light of truth and understand fully our actions and their effects. At that moment, we judge ourselves, estimate the worth of our deeds, and our suffering is a natural consequence of what we find out about ourselves.

But punishment isn't simply a condition of consciousness, remorse, or self-recrimination. There is an external component, as well. The Gita describes pain and toil, gloom and bewilderment, sinking into lower deeps, loaded with witlessness. Zoroaster also describes a life of darkness, foul food, and woeful wailing. Moses describes death and adversity in *this* life. Jesus describes everlasting fire and punishment. Krishna, Muḥammad, and Bahá'u'lláh describe different categories of punishment—higher and lower stations. While the path to misery is made easy, none but the most wretched are cast into the fire.

Perhaps we can compare these two aspects of punishment to the condition of a recovering drug addict or alcoholic who not only realizes the pain and suffering he has caused to those around him but also must face the fact that his choices have sapped his health and vitality, which may never be completely recovered. He must not only live with his remorse and knowledge of the pain he has inflicted on others but is also burdened with a body debilitated by his own choices and actions. In the same way, we find ourselves not only spiritually debilitated but also experiencing remorse and sorrow as we face the consequences of our deeds.

The Reward

While avoidance of punishment is one reason to cultivate virtue, the reward for cultivating it should be reason enough.

Krishna promises that a soul fixed in truth goes to a place perfect and pure, of those who know all Truth, that these souls rise ever higher, that the fruits are true and sweet, and that "light brings light." Zoroaster's promised reward is similar: the followers of Truth are promised immortality and that their dwelling shall be light. Moses refers to the rewards of obedience in this life—literally life and prosperity, thriving, increasing, and enduring—rewards much needed by a people struggling to survive. Buddha says the righteous person rejoices both in this world and the next and rejoices even more when he goes to the good place. Christ speaks of a kingdom that has been "prepared for you from the foundation of the world . . . life eternal." Muḥammad promises that those who fear God and assent to the good shall be well content and the path to happiness made easy. Bahá'u'lláh tells us of a joy and gladness impossible to describe and bonds of intimacy and fellowship with other souls of the same grade and station.

There is a temptation here to consider these rewards as a type of delayed gratification. I do the thing I don't like in order to acquire the thing I like. When I was a child, I liked spaghetti better than meatballs and frosting better than cake. I had to eat the meatballs if I wanted the spaghetti, and there was no way my mother would have let me have frosting without a slice of cake beneath it. So I ate the meatballs or the cake first—got it over with, so to speak—in order to lose myself in the pleasure of spaghetti or the unadulterated creamy frosting. To get to my reward, I had to move through some things less pleasurable.

But that is too simplistic. As an adult, I compare these rewards more to healthy diet and exercise. I don't always want to exercise or eat what's good for me. But when I do, I reap the rewards of improved health and of feeling my best. And I don't have to wait long for those rewards, either. When my health improves, I reach a *condition* of health. Living in a healthy manner becomes habituated, and health becomes my natural state.

So it is with spiritual values, with spiritual health. To work toward virtuous development creates happiness and contentment *now*. And, we are told, it leads to happiness and contentment later, as well. Truly it is a win-win situation.

Reading between the Lines

I suspect the rewards and punishments described cannot all be taken literally. After all, it's hard to understand what kind of threat hellfire or foul food can be to an entity without a body. Even so, rewards and punishments that are essentially spiritual in nature demand a physical description in order for us—physical creatures that we are—to grasp their nature. We cannot relate to the spiritual world and have no way of understanding it (except through the lens of virtue), as it lies beyond the limitations of the human plane of existence. And while physical descriptions cannot actually be applied to a non-physical reality, it is all we have. I believe, therefore, that the descriptions are designed to illustrate the quality of the experience and not the actual experience.

Also the places—such as heaven, hell, an unlighted womb, a perfect and pure place, the kingdom—are likely not places but conditions. In a nonmaterial world, "place" becomes irrelevant, as does "time" or any other quality (hot, cold, hard, soft) relating to the material world.

I notice from these scriptures that ignorance, darkness, evil, death, and hell are used interchangeably, as are knowledge, light, goodness, life, and heaven. Therefore, hell, a dark place of death and suffering, can also be a description of a lower station, as Bahá'u'lláh describes, of one who suffers knowing he or she has done evil. And heaven, a place of light and immortality, can be equated with a higher station, the souls one associates with in the next world, or a proximity to God and great joy.

Whatever the punishment or reward, it makes perfect sense when considered from a historical and cultural perspective. During most of human history, people understood the world very differently than we do today. When I place the life of Moses in the historic timeline, I realize that He led the Israelites to nationhood during the Bronze Age. This is a stupefying realization, actually, when I think of how differently the Israelite and I understand the world. The sciences by which I have learned to describe the world did not exist until very recently.

The Israelites, as well as the entire human population at the time, had no scientific explanation for things. The world over, crop failures, earthquakes, plagues, weather, health, and illness were explained in terms of rewards, curses, demonic possession, and the whims of gods and other supernatural beings. There was no knowledge of lands and peoples across the ocean. People had no mental image of the Earth as a sphere. Instead the moon, sun, and planets circled a fixed and flat Earth. Explanations and descriptions abounded to explain the heavens, stars, planets, day and night, and the turning of the seasons, not one of which can be called scientific. The art of writing was still developing and was a skill generally confined to scribes and priests. Most of the population was illiterate.

From the Torah, we have an account of the extreme severity of conditions for Moses and the Israelites. Life was harsh, and physical survival a top priority. Plagues, the weather, tenuous relationships with neighbors, as well as internal conflicts, the failure or success of a crop, the health of a herd—so many factors completely out of the Israelites' control—could have annihilated them as a people. Moses delivered a promise and a threat that people living under such circumstances could immediately relate to. He promised life and increase (prosperity) if they conformed to God's law, and He threatened them with harsh punishment, adversity, and death (something they were already too familiar with) if they disobeyed.

These threats and promises were literally true, and history bears this out. Had the Israelites turned fractious and lawless, the culture would certainly have dissolved before it got started. Adherence to the laws of Moses united these people into a cohesive whole and allowed them to prosper and thrive. Adherence to the laws also put them on the path of virtuous development, helped turn them into good people, and put them on the path to immortality as promised in other scriptures.

By the time of Christ, things had changed. Jewish culture had blossomed. Physical survival was no longer a daily pressure, and the promise of abundance or the threat of death no longer held as much immediacy or sting. Besides, by that time it was probably evident to most Jewish observers that many people, like their pagan Roman rulers who did not obey the directives of Moses, could live long and prosperous lives anyway.

The concept of eternal life was not revolutionary to the Jewish mind. (Jesus told the parable of the Good Samaritan when a Jewish lawyer tested Him by asking Him how to inherit eternal life.) Jesus urged His listeners to focus less on the rewards of this life and have faith in the rewards of the next life. So that they might gain those rewards, Jesus essentially asked no more of His followers than what Moses had asked of His: to love your neighbor as yourself.

The same description of rewards and punishments, only slightly altered to fit the Arab mindset, was also given by Muḥammad. Hellfire, to the unlettered Arabs of Muḥammad's day, was an effective threat. The path to happiness (identified as "Paradise" in other parts of the Koran) was also an enticing reward.

From Krishna we find punishments that describe pain, toil, gloom, and bewilderment. The idea of being born anew in some unlighted womb is a chilling one.* A soul fixed in truth rises higher, while darkened souls sink to lower depths. The idea is that "like brings like," a concept that Buddha reinforces when He declares that the righteous man rejoices both in this world and the next, knowing he has done good, while the evil-doer grieves in this world and suffers even more in the next.

The point is that we don't need a physical body to experience suffering or joy.

And, as already discussed, not all punishments are described as being delivered from an external source. They are also described as the result of our own understanding about our actions, as our self-imposed rationalizations become stripped away and we see our conduct for what it is.

Thus we grieve or rejoice. We can experience joy impossible to describe, or we can be seized by great fear and trembling. And so, while hellfire is synonymous with a torment, part of that torment can certainly be the result of our own judgment. But whatever the punishments describe, they all convey the same message: "This is the result of your own choices and something you'd rather avoid."

Darkness or Light

No matter how the guidance is worded, we are forced to circle back to the irrefutable priority of virtuous development. If we do this, we are essentially preparing ourselves to enter the place of light—heaven—to attain immortality, escape suffering, and attain to the higher ranks. We are given steps and instructions on how to do this. The Manifestations of God have described to Their respective audiences in the clearest terms the consequences for not engaging in the process and trying their utmost.

If we follow one path, very good things result. If we follow the other, very bad things result. While some of these rewards and punishments may be experienced in this world, others await until a later time, a time after physical death.

The next world. This is all, really, about preparation for that world.

The Manifestations of God tell us what steps we need to take so that we may enter the next world in a spiritually robust condition. Neglect of these steps leaves us spiritually unhealthy, unprepared, and underdeveloped. Loaded with spiritual "birth defects," we will find ourselves tossed into the ocean of light without the means to swim.

---

* It should be noted that in both Hindu and Buddhist tradition, reincarnation is a form of punishment, as it brings us back to a life inherently full of suffering. From this point of view, life *is* hell, and the goal is to escape the cycle of rebirth.

And here I find the answer to the question I posed at the time of my father's dying: how does one prepare for the inescapable moment of death that each of us must face? By diligently learning and applying what the Manifestations of God teach us, by exchanging, bit by bit, our false beliefs for truth. It is by constantly putting knowledge into action and doing our best to do good that we embrace life fully and prepare ourselves for what is to come.

14

Divine Revelation

Over the years, studying the writings of Bahá'u'lláh has become much like following a treasure map. Or maybe I should call it a Treasure Map, because the riches and gems I discover are of unsurpassed worth compared to the mere mineral variety. They are the latent "gems of inestimable value"[1]—my human potential yet to be made manifest. Through Bahá'u'lláh's writings my footsteps have been guided from one discovery to the next; as I travel I accumulate knowledge and understanding. This type of wealth never weighs me down and can never be taken from me. Through it I have found liberation, because I no longer need to wonder about who is a trustworthy authority to guide me. I have gained an understanding of the purpose of life, superlative goals, and a standard of behavior to strive toward that outshines any other.

As with any treasure map, one must follow it and make the necessary journey in order to find the treasure. While one can follow this map without physical travel, it is, nevertheless, an adventurous journey. While it is an interior journey, on it I have encountered villains, friends, foes, ogres, tyrants, and gods as I have closely examined my own beliefs, hopes, fears, and values, and faced them head-on.

Let's follow just a small part of that map and see what treasures we find. As I read the book *Gleanings from the Writings of Bahá'u'lláh*, I came across the following passage:

All praise and glory be to God Who, through the power of His might, hath delivered His creation from the nakedness of nonexistence, and clothed it with the mantle of life. From among all created things He hath singled out for His special favor the pure, the gem-like reality of man, and invested it with a unique capacity of knowing Him and of reflecting the greatness of His glory. This twofold distinction conferred upon him hath cleansed away from his heart the rust of every vain desire, and made him worthy of the vesture with which his Creator hath deigned to clothe him. It hath served to rescue his soul from the wretchedness of ignorance.[2]

My attention is caught at first by the reference to gems: "the gem-like reality of man." As I examine the context, it strikes me that this is a short description of the evolution of the universe that shows a progression of the universe coming into being and becoming adorned with life, and the singling out of the human being for the unique capacity to know God and reflect His glory.

My thoughts can roam in any direction in this short passage, as I picture the birth of the universe and its being literally covered with life. But it is the subject of humanity's being singled out for a special capacity that most interests me. For here it is plainly stated that the purpose of human existence is to know God and to reflect His glory. In fact, Bahá'u'lláh goes on to say:

This robe with which the body and soul of man hath been adorned is the very foundation of his well-being and development. Oh, how blessed the day when, aided by the grace and might of the one true God, man will have freed himself from the bondage and corruption of the world and all that is therein, and will have attained unto true and abiding rest beneath the shadow of the Tree of Knowledge![3]

Here I find not only that my purpose is to know God and to reflect His glory but also that my well-being and development depend upon it. This understanding needs to be my very foundation, the base upon which my entire life is built. Knowledge will grant me both freedom from corruption and abiding rest. Not just any knowledge can rescue me from ignorance, however—only knowledge of God.

As I study Bahá'u'lláh's writings, I come upon many descriptions of humanity's place and purpose in the scheme of things. For example, I read:

All things, in their inmost reality, testify to the revelation of the names and attributes of God within them. Each according to its capacity, indicateth, and is expressive of, the knowledge of God. So potent and universal is this revelation, that it hath encompassed all things visible and invisible. . . . Man, the noblest and most perfect of all created things, excelleth them all in the intensity of this revelation, and is a fuller expression of its glory. And of all men, the most accomplished, the most distinguished, and the most excellent are the Manifestations of the Sun of Truth. Nay, all else besides these Manifestations, live by the operation of their Will, and move and have their being through the outpourings of Their grace.[4]

Here Bahá'u'lláh tells us that while humanity's revelation of the attributes of God excels all others, the Manifestations of God's revelation excels even humanity's. But even beyond this, we all live and move by the outpourings of Their grace.

If this is true, it means we are dependent upon the Manifestations of God, and not just one of Them, but all of Them. According to Bahá'u'lláh, those who prefer one Manifestation of God above another are making a grave mistake. Bahá'u'lláh, in fact, often addresses the topic of God's Manifestations and takes great pains to educate us as to Their common mission.

I find this is a topic I must come to grips with if I want a full understanding of the purpose of my life. These are the Educators, after all, by Whose instruction I can reach my full potential. The Manifestations of God represent a critical piece of the puzzle. Bahá'u'lláh writes,

In thine esteemed letter thou hadst inquired which of the Prophets of God should be regarded as superior to others. Know thou assuredly that the essence of all the Prophets of God is one and the same. Their unity is absolute. God, the Creator, saith: There is no distinction whatsoever among the Bearers of My Message. They all have but one purpose; their secret is the same secret. To prefer one in honor to another, to exalt certain ones above the rest, is in no wise to be permitted. Every true Prophet hath regarded His Message as fundamentally the same as the Revelation of every other Prophet gone before Him. If any man, therefore, should fail to comprehend this truth, and should consequently indulge in vain and unseemly language, no one whose sight is keen and whose understanding is enlightened would ever allow such idle talk to cause him to waver in his belief.[5]

Here Bahá'u'lláh makes clear that the Manifestations of God have but one purpose. He also forbids considering one superior to another, a pitfall humanity repeatedly falls into. Every sentence in this passage, I find, is a doorway into myriad possibilities. But at this particular moment, what catches my attention is the reference to "secret." What is the secret that They all share? Does this refer to where They get Their knowledge? Obviously none of Them have teachers. Are

THE UNIVERSE WITHIN US

They self-taught? How can someone just innately know something nobody else knows yet? Bahá'u'lláh tells us the Manifestations of God are from God and are the Bearers of His message. Is this where They get Their knowledge? From God?

I decide, on this particular phase of my treasure hunt, to take another look at the other scriptures. What do the other Manifestations of God have to say about Their own station and the source of Their knowledge?

As I search through the various scriptures, I discover a third universal theme. I find that They do indeed each claim the same source of knowledge, and each claims to be charged with a mission that originates from a divine source.

Krishna:
He who knows thus in its true nature My divine birth and works is not born again, when he leaves his body but comes to Me, O Arjuna.*6

Moses:
And the Lord continued, "I have marked well the plight of My people in Egypt and have heeded their outcry. . . . Come, therefore, I will send you to Pharaoh and you shall free My people, the Israelites, from Egypt."

But Moses said to God, "Who am I that I should go to Pharaoh and free the Israelites from Egypt?" And He said, "I will be with you; that shall be your sign that it was I who sent you. And when you have freed the people from Egypt, you shall worship God at this mountain."

Moses said to God, "When I come to the Israelites and say to them 'The God of your fathers has sent me to you,' and they ask me, 'What is his name?' what shall I say to them?" And God said to Moses, "Ehyeh-Asher-Ehyeh."† He continued, "Thus shall you say to the Israelites, 'Ehyeh sent me to you.'" 7

Zoroaster:
Here, one man alone has listened to our Decrees.
He is Spitama Zarathushtra.‡

---

* The Bhagavadgita is a conversation between Krishna and the warrior prince, Arjuna, immediately preceding battle.
† Variously translated as "I Am That I Am," "I Am Who I Am," "I Will Be What I Will Be."
‡ Another name for Zoroaster.

He is eager to proclaim
the glory of Mazda* and His Truth
so let him be blest with sweetness of speech.[8]

Gautama Buddha:
I am one who has transcended all, a knower of all,
Unsullied among all things, renouncing all,
By craving's ceasing freed. Having known this all
For myself, to whom should I point as teacher?

I have no teacher, and one like me
Exists nowhere in all the world
With all its gods, because I have
No person for my counterpart.

I am the Accomplished One in the world,
I am the Teacher Supreme.
I alone am a Fully Enlightened One
Whose fires are quenched and extinguished.

I go now to the city of Kasi†
To set in motion the Wheel of Dhamma‡
In a world that has become blind
I go to beat the drum of the Deathless.[9]

Jesus Christ:
All things are delivered unto me of my Father: and no man knoweth the
Son, but the Father; neither knoweth any man the Father, save the Son, and
he to whomsoever the Son will reveal him. Come unto me, all ye that labour
and are heavy laden, and I will give you rest. Take my yoke upon you, and
learn of me; for I am meek and lowly in heart: and ye shall find rest unto
your souls.[10]

---

* Zoroastrian name for God.

† Currently the city of Varanasi, India, situated on the Ganges River.

‡ The Pali equivalent for the Sanskrit "Dharma," meaning rule of duty or obligation, mode of
being.

Muḥammad:
By the star when it setteth,
Your compatriot erreth not, nor is he led astray,
Neither speaketh he from mere impulse.
The Koran is no other than a revelation revealed to him:
One terrible in power taught it him,
Endued with wisdom. With even balance stood he
In the highest part of the horizon:
Then came he nearer and approached,
And was at the distance of two bows, or even closer,—
And he revealed to his servant what he revealed.
His heart falsified not what he saw.
What! Will ye then dispute with him as to what he saw?[11]

Bahá'u'lláh:
O King! I was but a man like others, asleep upon My couch, when lo, the breezes of the All-Glorious were wafted over Me, and taught Me the knowledge of all that hath been. This thing is not from Me, but from One Who is Almighty and All-Knowing. And He bade Me lift up My voice between earth and heaven, and for this there befell Me what hath caused the tears of every man of understanding to flow. The learning current amongst men I studied not; their schools I entered not. . . . This is but a leaf which the winds of the will of thy Lord, the Almighty, the All-Praised, have stirred. Can it be still when the tempestuous winds are blowing? . . . His all-compelling summons hath reached Me, and caused Me to speak His praise amidst all people. I was indeed as one dead when His behest was uttered. The hand of the will of thy Lord, the Compassionate, the Merciful, transformed Me.[12]

These statements are almost impossible to misinterpret. Krishna says His birth is "divine." Zoroaster claims that God has blessed Him with "sweetness of speech" as it is only He who listens to God's decrees. Buddha describes Himself as "knower of all," fully enlightened, and says that no one like Him exists in the world. Moses declares God has sent Him on a mission. Christ claims that only He knows God. Muḥammad tells us that His knowledge has been revealed to Him by One "terrible in power." Bahá'u'lláh claims that His knowledge of "all that hath been" is not from Him, but from God.

I have learned here that each of the Manifestations of God claim the same source for Their knowledge. But what of it? People can make the same claim, but that doesn't make the claim true. I'm sure I can find a number of people who claim they can fly or become invisible, but that doesn't mean they can. So, the next thing we have to consider is whether these claims are true. There is much riding on these assertions, so we should lose no time in examining them and coming to terms with either their truth or their falseness. After all, each of them is either right or wrong.

To find the answer, we simply need to ask three questions: Were They lying? Were They delusional? Or were They telling the truth?

Of course, the first two possibilities are certainly the most convenient. If They *were* lying, then we could go on our way, business as usual. Yet sheer evidence constrains us from simply pronouncing Them charlatans. By studying Their lives, we learn that, as mysterious and singular as were Their actions, they were not consistent with those of someone who is trying to profit from the gullibility of others. Their lives were generally spent in poverty, and They were often persecuted. Really, They would have been better off remaining silent. There was no profit in it for any of Them.

Neither do They conform with the actions of someone suffering delusions of grandeur. Indeed, They have an unparalleled understanding of reality and urge Their followers to avoid those constructs of the human imagination, such as false gods, religious dogma, racism, and nationalism. Their teachings help people distinguish between reality and those human constructs. To decide that these men, informed as They were with reality, were suddenly misinformed when it came to Themselves is not only inconsistent, it smacks of convenience.

We are, in fact, faced with an intentional, direct, and clear declaration that Their actions and teachings have sprung from the divine, and from God. As always, They say exactly what They mean to say. The content never varies, even under threat of death.

But how can we know in our hearts that such seemingly fantastic assertions are true? This is where the real work begins. One needs to be willing to weigh the possibilities, think about the matter, and make a decision.

Jesus Christ said, "Ye shall know them by their fruits."[13] This simple test can, of course, be applied to everything and everyone. My father put it this way, "If it looks like a duck, and quacks like a duck, and swims like a duck, it's probably a duck." In other words, it is impossible to pretend for long to be something you are not. While words may confuse, actions tell all. A military genius proves the worthiness of this title through his military exploits. A great scientist makes important discoveries and advances our understanding of the world. Political leaders shape historic events. Artists and architects create and build.

History records the deeds of such people and the fruits of their labors. We remember Alexander the Great because he was, indeed, a conqueror. We remember Copernicus because he advanced astronomical knowledge. We remember Michelangelo for his extraordinary *David*. We remember Abraham Lincoln as the focal point during the Civil War and the emancipator of enslaved people in the United States.

We don't remember everyone kindly. The fruit of the labors of many are horrible indeed. Adolf Hitler and Joseph Stalin are just two names we remember with disgust.

In addition, if we endeavor to learn from an actual soldier, scientist, or artist, we find that our own knowledge, understanding, and effectiveness in that particular area increases. Every student of astronomy knows of Copernicus and how he advanced our understanding of the solar system, as well as the universe, by recognizing that the Earth is not at its center. A soldier can learn much from the strategies used by Alexander the Great. An aspiring sculptor can benefit from studying the works of Michelangelo.

In every age and place, a student of any discipline needs to learn from a master of that discipline. A master is known by his or her works. An impostor is quickly exposed by a simple lack of skill or knowledge.

We must look at the fruit produced by the Manifestations of God, Who claim that Their knowledge is from God. Do They personify virtuous and spiritual ascendancy in the same way the scientific genius personifies intellectual ascendancy? Do They display faith, simplicity, meekness, sacrifice, detachment, trust, patience, justice, compassion, and love in act and deed? When we follow Their directives, do we develop faith, simplicity, meekness, sacrifice, detachment, trust, patience, justice, compassion, and love in word and deed?

Now, if indeed we find Them to be virtuous and knowledgeable beyond compare, if we find our characters improved and our virtuous potential becoming expressed in right action, and by these tests we eliminate the possibility of deception and delusion, then we must accept that these Manifestations of God are telling the truth and that They are what They claim to be. What is gained by continuing to doubt?

Coming to terms with this truth is a process. After all, much interior landscape must be traversed and many monsters (fears) and false gods (false beliefs) dealt with on the journey. My own journey consists of much plodding, punctuated by moments of great clarity and insight. In regard to this particular subject, which relates directly to the authority of Bahá'u'lláh, my moment of insight happened in the following way.

I had been studying the writings of Bahá'u'lláh for about one and a half years and found that I agreed with most of what Bahá'u'lláh said. But not everything. Now and then I either didn't like or disagreed with what I read. In those cases I automatically assumed Bahá'u'lláh had gotten it wrong. Until one day, in thinking about it, a strange thought entered my head: "If you agree with Bahá'u'lláh ninety-five percent of the time, perhaps in that other five percent *you* are wrong."

I was shocked by that thought, but it also opened me up. After all, I was wrong about lots of things. It was a pivotal moment for me, and from that time onward I felt a deeper level of receptivity. I think, basically, in that moment my ego had stepped aside.

And, of course, since I am at heart an experimenter, I shortly thereafter performed an experiment. I decided to go through one day as if I'd never heard of Bahá'u'lláh or His teachings.

When I rose that morning, I shut my mind to all thoughts of Bahá'u'lláh and proceeded through the day as far as I could get. By noon I couldn't stand it anymore. It was as if all the light and joy had gone out of the day, along with the air from my lungs. Everything had lost its vitality, and a colorless pall hung heavy over every proceeding. It didn't feel like life at all, but more like a half-life.

I realized then that, while I like to understand everything, Bahá'u'lláh was not among the mysteries I could unravel. Nevertheless He had irrevocably affected my life at a vital level, so much so that to be without Him now felt like being half dead. Yet, for that morning, I conducted business pretty much the way I had only two years before. The changes that had been wrought in me were so dramatic that I began referring to my life before Bahá'u'lláh as "my previous lifetime." I now understood what people meant when they referred to being spiritually reborn.

From my experiment I reached two conclusions: First, I couldn't live without Bahá'u'lláh. And second, I did not *want* to live without Him.

I now understand that the Manifestations of God are not simply in an advanced condition to which others can attain (otherwise, they certainly would), but that They belong to a unique station quite separate and distinct from our own. This unique station is acknowledged by Their unique titles: Prophet of God, Son of God, Tathagata (Perfect One), Apostle of God, and Manifestation of God.

But what is it exactly that distinguishes the Manifestations of God from us? Obviously They share with us a physical existence. To this we can relate easily, as They experience the same physical needs and infirmities as the rest of us do. And while They are virtuously perfect, we, too, are virtuous, albeit imperfectly.

There *is* one power They possess that we do not, and this power, too, is referred to in all the scriptures. This unique power has evoked from humanity a myriad of responses—mystification, awe, wonder, belief, and even suspicion. This power, which distinguishes Them entirely, is the power of Divine Revelation.

Krishna:
I will declare to thee that utmost lore,
Whole and particular, which, when thou knowest,
Leaveth no more to know here in this world.[14]

Moses:
. . . Moses said to the Lord, "Please, O Lord, I have never been a man of words, either in times past or now that You have spoken to Your servant; I am slow of speech and slow of tongue." And the Lord said to him, "Who gives man speech? Who makes him dumb or deaf, seeing or blind? Is it not I, the Lord? Now go, and I will be with you as you speak and will instruct you what to say."[15]

Zoroaster:
Then I realised You as Bountiful,
O Mazda Ahura,
When the Good Mind encircled me.
When I first became enlightened through Your
inspired Words,
then I realised
that to do what is best for mankind
would cause me suffering.

Then You said to me:
"Go, instruct man in the Truth,
and reveal teachings hitherto unheard of."[16]

Gautama Buddha:
The Lord asked: What do you think, Subhuti, is there any dharma* which the Tathagata[†] has fully known as the utmost, right, and perfect enlightenment, or is there any dharma which the Tathagata has demonstrated? Subhuti

---

* Rule of duty or obligation, mode of being.
† A title of the Buddha meaning "He who has thus come."

replied: No, not as I understand what the Lord has said. And why? This dharma which the Tathagata has fully known or demonstrated—it cannot be grasped, it cannot be talked about, it is neither a dharma nor a non-dharma. And why? Because an Absolute exalts the Holy Persons.[17]

Jesus Christ:
For I have not spoken of myself; but the Father which sent me, he gave me a commandment, what I should say, and what I should speak.[18]

Muḥammad:
It is not for me to change [the Koran] as mine own soul prompteth. I follow only what is revealed to me. . .[19]

Bahá'u'lláh:
Not of Mine own volition have I revealed Myself, but God, of His own choosing, hath manifested Me. . . . Whenever I chose to hold My peace and be still, lo, the Voice of the Holy Spirit, standing on My right hand, aroused Me, and the Most Great Spirit appeared before My face, and Gabriel overshadowed Me, and the Spirit of Glory stirred within My bosom, bidding Me arise and break My silence.[20]

Here something extraordinary is being described. Krishna tells us that what He has to say will teach those who listen all they need to know in this world. Zoroaster calls His own teachings "hitherto unheard of." Moses is instructed by God what to say, which is made abundantly clear by His display of self-doubt. Christ tells us not only that His Father tells Him what to say but that He has been given a commandment to say it. In other words, He is being obedient to God by speaking. Muḥammad declares He is not the author of the Koran but follows only what is revealed to Him. Bahá'u'lláh speaks only because He is bidden to break His silence.

I took an analytical look at these descriptions of Divine Revelation and found the combination of two components. Their source is declared to be from God (thus the "divine"), and through this process we are taught that which was previously unknown to us (thus the "revelation"). What was once hidden and unknown now stands revealed.

When Buddha says that an "Absolute exalts the Holy Persons," that it is not a dharma or a non-dharma, He is telling us that the power of revelation cannot be learned, that an Absolute—defined by my dictionary as "something perfect, pure, independent, and without limits"—fills and raises up these holy persons.

THE UNIVERSE WITHIN US

By declaring the source of Their teachings to be God, They are also telling us that They Themselves are not the authors of what They reveal. Revelation comes through Them; it does not originate with Them.

Let's be perfectly clear that Divine Revelation is a completely different phenomenon from inspiration. Inspiration is usually experienced during a long process of study and contemplation. I find myself, from time to time, inspired. I was, perhaps, inspired to write this book, but that was only the beginning of the process, and this book is the result of many years of endeavor. The end result is not at all my original vision. It is both much vaster and much deeper. What it contains is contingent upon what I learned from both the sciences and the Manifestations of God. Everything I have written about is already known. I feel I have had a lot of assistance, from both this world and the next. I have never felt this book was entirely my own but that it was something that needed doing, if I could avail myself of all the resources available. Despite my best efforts, it is loaded with shortcomings, as am I. My synthesis of the information may be unique, but I am not revealing hitherto unknown realities. Inspired? Maybe. Revealed? Definitely not. Human beings can be inspired, but only the Manifestations of God can reveal.

That which is revealed often runs counter to cultural norms. There are always culturally specific ideas of right and wrong, good and bad. One culture may condone slavery. Another may advocate a belief in multiple gods. Another may promote human or animal sacrifices to appease those gods. A culture may be stratified into a rigid caste system. It may make prostitution legal. It may rationalize experimentation on animals. It may value physical strength in men and physical beauty in women. Perhaps it encourages competition over cooperation. A culture may reward those who kill in war and execute those who kill during peacetime.

Revelation cannot be contained within cultural mores, nor does it fit into societal norms. Divine Revelation is concerned with reality. When a Revelation is at odds with beloved values and conceptions, people react with fear, or anger, or ignore the Revelation altogether. People have many reasons and justifications for not wanting to change whatever system is in place. For example, people may argue that doing without slavery is inconvenient. Societies can become really fond of false gods and the institutions that spring up around them—never mind the jobs that might become obsolete if those institutions fail. Of course, if I am a member of the ruling class, I'm not going to like the idea of the equality of all people. And if I'm a big strong guy, used to getting my way through intimidation, or, as it might be considered, *competition*, I'm not going to be very quick to embrace the idea of cooperation. In short, asking people to give up whatever advantages they presently enjoy rarely goes over well.

Despite the immediate discomfort, objections, and inconveniences, we must examine our beloved conceptions and values so that we can identify and discard falsehood in exchange for understanding reality and the purpose of life. Only Divine Revelation initiates and supports this process.

We have found the source of the greatest treasure—that which will bring forth those gems of inestimable value latent within us. It is the Manifestations of God, Who call us from preoccupation with the material world and awaken us to our spiritual nature. Only Their Revelations can teach us how to translate that awakened spiritual consciousness into everyday action.

Divine Revelation has everything to do with what we are, what we are becoming, and how to realize our potential. Tender plants that we are, we must seek out the light and turn toward it. By orienting ourselves toward the Manifestations of God, we not only find ourselves facing the direction toward which we are developing, we find the source of nourishment that assists and accelerates the process that every adult should be most concerned with—the process of virtuous development.

As They speak of that portion of reality that we have yet to embrace, the Manifestations of God speak often in allegory, metaphor, and parable. Mysterious and rich in meaning, Their words offer us a multilayered conduit of elucidation and enlightenment. It is only by diligently studying and conforming to these teachings that we become increasingly able to distinguish our limited and incorrect concepts, move closer to reality, learn the true purpose of life, develop authentic selves, and become truly human.

15

Oneness

Because my mind craves order, I divide the world into categories: alive or dead, good or bad, friend or enemy, solid or liquid, mineral, vegetable, animal, and on and on.

On a deeper level, I divide it into powers: attraction, augmentation, intelligence (cognition and emotion), intellect, virtue, and Divine Revelation.

These divisions could be endless, as I am inclined to carve things into smaller and smaller pieces. They work as a type of map and help me negotiate the world. I make associations; I draw conclusions. When I find a pattern, I feel I have reached an understanding. I feel like I know something.

To this end, I've drawn a map of the universe based on capacity. I've extended that map somewhat based on what the Manifestations of God have told us.

But I cannot leave the world divided. These divisions, after all, are artificial. They are a concoction of the mind. They suit me and the way I look at things. They help me understand the world and my place and purpose in it.

But the world, in truth, is an indivisible whole. I want to understand the universe as that whole. I want to understand myself as part of that whole. I crave conscious reunion with the universe. I don't forever want to feel like I am on the outside looking in. Because the truth is, I am not outside of it looking in. I am inside of it, a living breathing part of it. I belong to this inseparable whole. I have been brought forth in this world, and I am affected by and affect it. When a vibration runs through it, I vibrate.

In order to come to grips with this, I must let all these divisions fall away—just allow things to be, for starters, without labeling them. I can think of it this way: reality is. The universe is what the universe is. There are no two ways about it. My divisions do not divide reality. My feelings of separation from it do not separate me from it. Reality is, ultimately, one reality. There can never be two realities, any more than there can be three or four realities.

Certainly we can have different opinions about reality. But those opinions have no effect on reality itself and cannot create different realities or truths. While I cannot avoid my point of view, I must also constantly remind myself that reality is one and indivisible. If I do not do this, I may begin to confuse my point of view, and my way of understanding, with reality. This is a mistake human beings make all too often.

But let's explore this juxtaposition of one indivisible reality and countless points of view. Surely there are examples in our everyday experience that can illustrate its meaning.

How about sunshine? We all know that sunshine comes from one source—the Sun. We have a variety of ways of comprehending the Sun. Rocks are warmed by it. Plants use it to perform the vital function of photosynthesis. Animals and most people begin and end their days according to either its rising or setting.

The Sun travels in an arc across the sky, a long trip in the summer, a shorter trip in winter. Then the Sun sinks below the horizon and people experience darkness. In the mid-latitudes, the sun rises and sets at different points on the horizon throughout the year. If you live at the equator, you experience roughly twelve hours of daylight and twelve hours of darkness. As you move closer to the poles, you will experience longer days and shorter nights in the summer. If you live close enough to the poles, you will even experience a period in which the Sun never sets. Likewise, in the winter, the length of days shortens and night increases until the winter solstice, a period of endless night.

What I just described is true in one sense, but untrue in another. While it describes the variety of ways people experience the Sun, in reality, the Sun doesn't rise or set at all. In reality, the Earth revolves and rotates, turning its inhabitants ever away from or toward the Sun, moving always along the course of its orbit. From the solar point of view, there is no rising or setting, there are no days or nights. A superheated mass of plasma, the Sun fuses hydrogen into helium, releasing a steady stream of light and heat in all directions into space.

But we who stand in its path experience that light and heat in a variety of ways. One Sun, but countless experiences of sunshine.

To find another example of oneness, I need look no further than my own life. My entire life is one indivisible process. I may categorize it by years, or by developmental phases, but those categories are artificial. I may categorize myself by different aspects—physical, intellectual, or spiritual—but these categories are also arbitrary. I am one indivisible human being that undergoes processes: spirit, intellect, and body, all seamlessly interconnected, all dimensions of one indivisible life.

And my life is part of a larger indivisible process of a developing humanity that, in turn, is part of the Earth's developmental process. We divide this process, too, in meaningful ways, into eras, epochs, and ages. It helps us understand history, both of the Earth and of ourselves, by creating categories such as Pliocene Epoch, Proterozoic Era, Jurassic Period, Bronze Age, or Middle Ages. We are in an era and age right now, too, I suppose, although those who will decide which period of time it represents and then label it are yet to be born. That particular label will suit the authors'—our descendants—points of view.

I have no idea how future generations will decide to carve things up, but it doesn't matter. The truth is, no matter how we might label things and divide history, everything and everyone—past, present, and future—is actually part of one indivisible reality, one indivisible universe, one indivisible Earth, and one indivisible process.

To this unified reality belongs all that is—all processes, capacities, and objects—whether sunlight, the development of planets and evolution of species, every creature in the universe, and every human being. I belong to it, as do you. Every Manifestation of God belongs to this unified reality. Our minds, our hearts, and our souls belong to it. Our ability to laugh and weep belong to it. Our ability to discover reality's secrets belong to it, as does our ability to produce great works of art. It's as if objects (even myself) and events are just temporary manifestations of this process-driven reality. Like waves on the surface of a vast ocean, they rise for a short time and sink again into the ocean's inseparable oneness.

Ultimately, because reality cannot be multiplied, the quest for knowledge of reality, pursued in an honest and fearless fashion, must lead each of us closer and closer to the same truth. This is why education works no matter where it takes place. There is not an arithmetic that works in the West but not in the East. Real mathematics works the world over. An accurate map of the world hanging on the wall in a Peruvian classroom will be identical to an accurate map hanging in a Kenyan classroom. Biological sciences belong to no particular land, and while particular species may be regional, the biological sciences can be applied anywhere. Thus education works, as long as that education is focused on the discovery of truth and on reality.

If the Manifestations of God are teachers of reality, teachers of truth, then what They teach must also be unified and be one and the same. Why, then, do adherents of different religions develop such animosity toward each other? Why are there such vast differences between those religions that develop in the wake of the Manifestations' Revelations, even to the point of schisms that develop within those religions?

We must consider the aspect of point of view, for, as discussed previously, while reality is singular, points of view are without limit. To illustrate this, let's look at a scenario that is less emotionally charged than religion. This is the scenario of two math teachers: Jo, the Best Math Teacher Ever, and Li, the Greatest Math Educator in the World.

Jo and Li

Jo, a math teacher in the port city of Goswana, has earned the reputation of being the Best Math Teacher Ever. He is the inventor of a new kind of abacus with which he teaches addition, subtraction, multiplication, division, and algebra. Algebra is an advance in mathematics unheard of previously. Prior to Jo's invention, no abacus could perform the calculations.

Algebra turns out to be a baffling subject for most of his students, but some do very well with it. Some become great engineers and builders, and others go on to teach mathematics. As for the rest, this is a seaport city run by merchants, and the ability to accurately and quickly tally figures is in great demand.

There are five abacuses in his classroom, and Jo assigns groups of students to each abacus. In the early part of the day, the groups are composed of older and younger students, and the older must teach the younger. In the latter part, the older and younger students separate in order to concentrate on their own level of study.

Jo always makes himself available, sometimes wandering from group to group to check on their progress, sometimes sitting in his corner and letting his students come to him. Since the climate is warm and dry, his students study from dawn until lunchtime, when temperatures are amenable. They leave their sandals outside and sit on a sandy floor. The windows are open to the outside air to let the refreshing morning breeze pass through. Jo's classroom is noisy. Students mill about, helping each other with their problems, or looking for help.

Jo lives around the corner from a candy maker and has gotten into the habit of bringing in sesame-honey candy once a month to share with his students.

His students are, alas, only boys. In this culture, it is believed that only boys have the capacity for such intellectual challenges. Girls need only learn about what will serve them as wives and mothers.

Some boys, however, share what they learn with their sisters. Parents find this acceptable, since the sister can never learn more than her brother that way. Besides, this knowledge could help make her more marriageable, as she will be able to help her husband keep his business records. Now and then, a student brings his sister's questions to Jo. Along with his answer, Jo has been known to send some of these girls a piece of sesame-honey candy to show his pleasure and approval.

So revered is Jo that after his death a university is founded by some of his former students in his name, dedicated to the study of mathematics. They call it the University of Jo. On the wall by the front door is a carved marble plaque proclaiming: "Dedicated to Jo, the Best Math Teacher Ever."

It is not a large school, just a few rooms built in the style of Jo's classroom: open windows, sandy floors, and abacuses. Sandals are left at the door. Once a month, a teacher brings in sesame-honey candy to distribute. It's a casually run school.

Attendance starts off small but increases over the years, and an addition is eventually built. A hundred years later, a new building is put up to meet growing demand. Two hundred years later, the school has grown to such a size that a whole administrative order is employed just to run it. As the institution grows in size, power, and influence, hierarchies evolve, presidents are appointed, boards are elected, and faculty is hired.

Pretty soon the university is run by folks who, while they aren't necessarily great mathematicians, are very competent administrators. They institute a variety of policies necessary for operating this growing institution, such as fees, graduation requirements, dress codes, disciplinary penalties, class schedules, teacher credentials, and so on.

During this time, the first girls' school opens. This school began in the back room at the home of one of the girls who learned math from her brother. She began to teach it to her friends, and somehow it kept going. She was a very good teacher, and her friends and neighbors often sent their daughters to her for instruction.

After her death, some of her students decide to open their own school. At first, facing objections, they argue that Jo's gift of the sesame candy to his students' sisters signified his implied approval of math education for girls. Slowly, the school gains acceptance, and eventually, it becomes common practice for girls to receive this type of instruction, although they continue to learn only at girls' schools, which are staffed and taught strictly by women.

As the centuries roll by at the University of Jo, more and more mathematical treatises are published by the many brilliant minds that are produced by this center of learning. Many of these authors are also university professors who develop courses around their own specialized area of study. Over time, these become more and more popular and gradually come to take primary importance in the curriculum.

There are some people who do not like the changes that have developed over the centuries. They feel strongly that people have strayed too far from the simplicity of Jo's mathematics education and want to revive it. The problem is that Jo left very little behind about his education philosophy. There is only the *Anthology*, basically interviews of Jo's friends and neighbors. This book is full of stories about Jo, but it isn't really helpful for setting up a school.

They find more useful a book by Eb, a student of Jo's. Eb was instrumental in founding the original school after Jo's death. They turn to this book for their primary guidance and set up a new math school. They name it "School of Jo's Fundamentals."

Of course, how much this school reflects Jo's actual mathematical and teaching philosophy is anybody's guess. It is a school actually founded on Eb's philosophies, and, while Eb claimed to be Jo's star pupil, historians can't actually validate the truth of this claim. Nevertheless the school thrives, and soon many other schools form, not so Eb-centered, perhaps, but still independent of the central and most powerful college institution.

A thousand years have now passed since Jo's death. Rumors are beginning to circulate about a new math teacher who lives far to the north. His name is Li, and some people are calling Li the Greatest Math Educator in the World. As these rumors grow, some of the Jo scholars become curious enough to decide to investigate.

They travel over a thousand miles north to a mountainous rural area, where their inquiries lead them to the outskirts of a small town. There the Jo scholars find Li and introduce themselves to him as mathematicians.

Li welcomes them warmly.

The Jo scholars tell him that his fame has reached their land and that they have journeyed a great distance to meet him in order to corroborate these rumors. They ask to observe his classroom and his teaching method, and Li consents.

They are surprised when he tells them school does not begin until midmorning, as the children come from surrounding farms and have chores to do before they can come to school. Such a late hour! (It had long ago been conclusively established that beginning lessons at an early hour is the key to successful learning, and Li's method of not starting until midmorning gets some of the scholars grumbling.)

The scholars arrive ten minutes before the students are due to arrive. The classroom is actually just a converted storehouse in Li's backyard. It is strangely set up, they observe. No sandy floors here, no open windows, not even an abacus in sight! Instead, they find the windows glazed and a potbellied stove in the corner, which

Li has just lit. (The benefits of fresh air to the learning process had also been long proven and are accepted as simple common sense. The scholars are beginning to feel doubtful indeed.)

Li explains that the glazing keeps the cold out and the visitors can surely appreciate the warmth of the stove. Strange as all this seems, the scholars concede that, while unusual, it is certainly reasonable. They definitely appreciate the warmth beginning to bellow from the stove and gather round it.

Their eyes next fall upon the rows of wooden benches and then on the stack of slates in the front of the room alongside a box full of pieces of chalk. At the back of the classroom hangs a large piece of slate. They've never seen slate or chalk and can't imagine what they are for.

"And where are the abacuses?" asks one scholar.

"There are no abacuses," Li replies. "Only slate and chalk."

If they were surprised at the setup of Li's classroom, they are positively shocked at this. No abacuses? And he calls himself a mathematician? Has their journey been wasted?

Li explains that his math is done by equations and formulas. The chalk and slate are all his students need to perform their calculations.

The Jo scholars are doubtful.

And if they are shocked at the absence of abacuses, they become nearly apoplectic at the next turn of events. As the students begin to arrive, the scholars see that they are both boys and girls! As each student arrives, he or she greets Li, picks up a piece of chalk and slate, and sits down on a bench. Boys and girls, all intermingled in the same classroom, on the same bench!

Some of the scholars have seen quite enough, thank you, and depart in a huff. The rest, although decidedly uncomfortable, decide to stick it out. And a few scholars, who have always felt that girls are quite as capable as boys, are beginning to thoroughly enjoy this visit.

In Li's classroom silence is the rule, for the most part, to aid in concentration. His students work their calculations on their slates, scribbling with their pieces of chalk. At the large slate in the back, the older students work on more complex equations.

Li wanders around the classroom and kindly aids those struggling with a particular problem. He checks students' progress and discusses possible solutions to their difficulties. At the end of an hour, he has the students stand, and they perform a stretching routine he has taught them that gets their blood flowing.

There is also a period of singing. Li has composed a song by which the younger students memorize their multiplication table. The song goes in rounds, and the sound of their voices circulates around the room and meshes into a wonderful melody.

All of Li's students obviously enjoy this exercise, as the wide grins on their faces testify. It is a challenge to keep the rounds going, and they are not always successful, but it is always fun.

The Jo scholars find this music strange (where they come from, now that's *real* music), and some wonder privately whether the classroom is an appropriate place for singing. They don't like the quiet of the classroom (so different is it from the gabble and noise they are used to), and to have it punctuated by this stretching and singing is very disconcerting indeed.

At the end of two hours, it is time for lunch. The students sit on their benches, eat their bagged lunches, then go outside (weather permitting) to play and run around a bit. When they come back inside, they are ready to continue their lessons.

The scholars take note of something interesting going on at the back slate. Li tells them that it is called calculus, a new type of math that involves algebra but is more advanced and can be used to measure things like rate of change.

They can hardly believe their ears! A few scholars are intrigued, but the others can't imagine needing anything more than algebra.

The scholars depart for home in a fractious and discontented state. Arguments erupt between them.

Can you believe that classroom? Who can learn with closed windows?

What do windows matter? Clearly they are learning mathematics.

Without an abacus? Is it really mathematics without an abacus?

Those equations have taken the place of the abacus.

Well, I like my abacus. Mine has been passed down from father to son for generations, and I would never give it up for a worthless piece of chalk and slate!

And did you notice? No sesame-honey candy. I asked, and he never heard of it!

And how about that calculus business? What a waste of time. We've been functioning for a thousand years with algebra and have designed everything from buildings to bridges with it. How can calculus add to that?

And how about those girls? Girls! Next thing you know, they'll want to attend university!

Well, what's wrong with girls in the classroom with boys? It's high time they have the same opportunities.

It will be the ruin of them! And this title people call him by: "Greatest Math Educator in the World." How ridiculous! We've got the only Best Math Teacher Ever. Ever!

"Well," says one discerning scholar, "the important thing is that they are learning mathematics. Despite the different circumstances and their unfamiliar ways, it is undoubtedly mathematics. Isn't that the important thing? And no one even asked Master Li the practical application for calculus."

His voice is drowned out in a deluge of protests, and he walks on in silence. But he forms in his heart a plan to write to Master Li (for so he now calls him) to ask for the uses of calculus. If he is satisfied by the answer, perhaps he will even ask to be allowed to study under him.

And so it goes. Instead of recognizing and focusing on the oneness of the founding principle—mathematics—the Jo scholars focus on the different practices without considering that they are merely incidental.

Jo lived in a merchant town where extroversion was encouraged, and he was himself outgoing and gregarious. Li lived in a farming society and was of a more introspective nature. Jo left the windows open because he lived in an amenable climate. Li closed the windows and lit a stove to keep warm. Their teaching styles, of course, reflect their personalities. Jo's students started early because in that warm climate, mornings are the most congenial time of day. Li's students began later because they had early-morning farm chores to complete. Jo modified the abacus already familiar to his people. Li used slate because slate was available. And it was possible for Li to introduce calculus because the algebra that Jo had taught was now widespread and well-known.

Religion and the Manifestations of God

While greatly oversimplified, scenarios such as the story of Jo and Li can be applied to the major religions.

A Manifestation of God appears. His reputation spreads, and He attracts those souls who yearn for spiritual truth. He also attracts deprecators, those people attached to their traditions and their own understanding of scripture.

The Manifestation of God lays down laws and teachings. His followers comprehend and apply them, each according to his or her capacity and willingness. In other words, there is the Revelation, and there is how each of us responds to that Revelation. Some will go on to become famous teachers and promoters of the Revelation, while others will become improved in more subtle ways.

After the death of the Manifestation of God, over a period of time, institutions begin to evolve around the preservation and promulgation of the Revelation. Not everything is wonderful. Human nature is, after all, human nature. Power-seekers will take advantage of any available situation, be it business, politics, or religion.

Power struggles often erupt, with control of the institutions going to the winner. The resulting fallout often creates multiple schisms, with differing views about the application of these teachings.

Nevertheless, despite internal disputes and external persecutions, the new religion takes anchor, spreads roots, and becomes firmly established. Many hearts are truly inspired, and people work with renewed energy and direction.

Society undergoes a revitalization; civilization blossoms and advances. How this religion is expressed—its ceremonies, its rules, and the architecture of its buildings—is shaped by circumstances we can only call incidental. That is, the spiritual impulse will be expressed in ways specific to the culture. Eventually— perhaps centuries later—and inevitably, the religion reaches its zenith of ascendancy and experiences a time of great predominance and influence.

By this time, institutions and administrations have become well established. Worship is, by now, ritualized, institutions and hierarchies have become fixed, and a religious elite—clergy and scholars—have become the accepted interpreters of scripture. Teachers of different calibers come and go, and some are so amazingly erudite and wise that small subcultures, or denominations, spring up based on each teacher's particular philosophy. Splits within the religion can occur at any time and often spring from disagreements about the meaning of scripture.

In fact, over time, Divine Revelation can become so clouded by human interpretation of scripture and the addition of human-authored texts that many religious adherents do not know which of their scriptures are divinely revealed and which are the product of an inspired human author.

Often, human-authored scripture is given ascendancy over the original Revelation. Thus many Christians adhere more closely to Paul's teachings than to Christ's. Much of Buddhist scripture is, unabashedly, not attributed to Buddha at all. The Krishna of Hinduism is lost in a cloud of antiquity, relegated to the role of a mythical figure, one god from a pantheon of gods. Jewish scripture, too, has expanded well beyond the Torah.

All of this is going on within the religion: ups, downs, intrigues, power struggles, emerging leadership, schisms, expansion, advancement, arguments, agreements, all and everything that people do, both wonderful and vile.

And then . . . a new Manifestation of God appears. His mission? To revivify humanity's desire for self-knowledge, spiritual growth, truth, and authenticity. He redirects our vision away from the incidental and the cultural—rituals and rites, laws and institutions—and directs us back to truth and reality, back to the heart and purpose of human existence. Those who yearn for spiritual truth turn to Him, and the cycle begins anew.

The appearance of each Manifestation of God, as separate and singular as it may have seemed in the past, in truth belongs to one indivisible and unified process. Their purpose is but one—to educate, illumine, and inspire human virtue, and to manifest humankind's spiritual potential on the material plane. Wherever They have appeared, this has certainly been the result. As individuals do not live in a vacuum, society is consequently improved when this happens. As individuals develop and evolve, so, inevitably, does civilization.

The repeating appearances of the Manifestations of God are mentioned in the world's sacred texts. There is general consensus as to the repetition, if not how it comes about. In the Bhagavad Gita, Lord Krishna tells us that He appears whenever righteousness declines and wickedness is strong, in order to succor the good and reestablish virtue. In the book of Isaiah, we are told of One to be born called "Wonderful," "Counselor," and "Prince of Peace." Zoroastrian scripture foretells the coming of a "Sháh-Bahrám" or World Savior. Buddhists believe in the future appearance of the Maitreya Buddha, a supremely enlightened holy One. Christ warns His followers to be on the lookout for the Spirit of Truth who will guide humanity to all truth. Islamic tradition foretells the appearance of the Mihdí (One Who Is Guided) who will appear at a time of God's choosing. Bahá'u'lláh also refers to a future Manifestation of God and tells us that another will appear after the expiration of one thousand years from the time of His own ministry.[1]

The Progression of Divine Revelation

Divine Revelation is necessarily tempered by humanity's capacity to comprehend what is being revealed. In school you were taught how to add and subtract before being taught how to multiply and divide. To learn any of the higher math functions, you first had to learn the basics of addition and subtraction. And one must master algebra before moving on to calculus. All learning, including spiritual learning, is progressive in this way.

Each Manifestation of God expands the scope of Revelation according to humanity's capacity as a whole. This capacity should not be confused with immediate receptivity and readiness. It can take, minimally, until the appearance of the next Manifestation of God for such teachings to spread and to become accepted as truth.

Take the practice of slavery, for example. During most of history, slavery was an institutionalized practice, sanctioned by society and government and regulated by laws. It was an accepted mode of economics, much as capitalism is an accepted system of economics in the West today.

Had Moses or Muḥammad attempted to abolish the practice of slavery, how successful would They have been? Indeed, the fact that They did not reflects only the human condition: we were not ready for it.

Instead, Moses and Muḥammad improved the condition and treatment of slaves. This is only wisdom, as most people would not have been able to handle the idea of completely abolishing the practice. But to take a small step and humanize the treatment of slaves prepared the way for the eventual abolishment of slavery.

In fact, both the abolition of slavery and the equality of women have finally been pronounced by Bahá'u'lláh. Yet, even now, how many willingly embrace these pronouncements? Slavery is—finally—no longer a legally sanctioned practice, yet it continues to exist in many places in the world.

As for the equality of women and men, in those places where equality is paid lip service, laws are needed to ensure opportunity as well as protection. In other parts of the world, the equality of women with men is not even a consideration.

Each Manifestation of God knows the same truth, for truth is reality, and reality is singular. But, as a teacher in first grade will teach addition and withhold the more complex principles of multiplication for a later time, so does each Manifestation of God reveal only what is timely and appropriate and only that which serves the current educational needs of an evolving humanity.

Thus it is only now that slavery has been abolished and the equality of women and men has been pronounced. It is only now that we are taught the oneness of God, the oneness of God's Manifestations, and the oneness of religion.

The appearances of the Manifestations of God may be incredible events, yet these appearances belong to a seamless unified process that Bahá'u'lláh calls "progressive Revelation." In this context, He describes religions as "dispensations," periods of time representing different phases of humanity's evolution.[2]

That the religions actually represent one unfolding religion of God is a reality never before revealed to us. Many have suspected that religions are unified by a common thread, but it is Bahá'u'lláh Who has finally enlightened us on this subject, completely solving this former puzzle. With the global view before us, we can now grasp how these apparently separate pieces join to form a whole.

The fact is, humanity is one people, this planet is one planet, this world is one world. This one world has progressed and developed and continues now to progress and develop. This one human species progresses and develops, too. Our group identity has progressed over the past six thousand years from family to clan to tribe to kingdom to empire to nation. From family to empire, we have identified ourselves according to ethnicity, religion, and culture.

But today, people have moved around the planet, taking up residence in new lands. There is a great mixing of populations, the scope of which has no historical precedent. Nations today do not enjoy traditional and ancient commonalities, and citizens of the same country find themselves elbow-to-elbow with people of different ethnicities, religions, and cultures. We find ourselves struggling to come to grips with what it means to be an American, an Iraqi, an Israeli, a Russian, a Christian, a Chinese, a Muslim—a human being.

We are on the verge of recognizing the arbitrary categories we have created. We are beginning to distinguish the incidental and accidental nature of national boundaries, cultures, and religions. We are on the verge of recognizing the fundamental oneness of humanity, the oneness of the world, and the oneness of the process that has brought us all, willingly or not, to this point in the process—a point that will irrevocably establish the unity of all humankind.

16

God

I was once asked by a college-educated Christian, "Which God do Bahá'ís believe in?"

I asked in return, "How many Gods are there?"

"One," she answered.

To which I replied, "That's the One."

I was taken aback by the question. As a Catholic, I had been raised a monotheist, and I thought that *all* Christians were monotheists. Indeed, her answer to my question proved that she believed in the existence of only one God. In that case, where had her question come from?

Now and then, I come across that same puzzling idea. A few years ago, I heard a Christian on the radio declare, "The Muslim God is not *my* God." *What is this about?* I asked myself. *Could this actually be a subconscious admission to belief in multiple gods?*

No, I don't think so. I think it is actually a statement about names and definitions. We may confuse the name with the Object. Believing that different names represent different entities, we may conclude that others worship a false god.

In addition, the descriptions of God from other religions may sound so strange that we have a hard time reconciling it with our own understanding. Of course, can any finite being describe or comprehend the Infinite? I think not. Yet, when our incomplete, inaccurate, and paltry descriptions clash, instead of acknowledging our limitations, we stand proudly by our own flawed definition and cast aspersions toward others.

Let's be absolutely clear about this. God cannot fit into our own measly descriptions. God cannot fit into our imaginations. God is too grand, too vast, and just too big for anything we might be able to imagine and assign words to.

While the signs of God permeate all levels of existence (we have certainly witnessed this as we have moved from one level of existence to the next), the essence and nature of God is the most elusive and abstruse mystery of all.

The Manifestations of God have addressed this subject in contexts best suited to Their respective audiences and thus use a variety of approaches. These differing perspectives may appear, at first, contradictory, yet the variety of ways to describe the Infinite must also be infinite.

I present them here for your consideration.

Krishna:

By Me all this universe is pervaded through My unmanifested form. All beings abide in Me but I do not abide in them. And (yet) the beings do not dwell in Me; behold My divine mystery. My spirit which is the source of all beings sustains the beings but does not abide in them. . . . Under My guidance, Nature gives birth to all things, moving and unmoving, and by this means . . . the world revolves. . . . I am the father of this world, the mother, the supporter, and the grandsire. I am the object of knowledge, the purifier. . . . I am the goal, the upholder, the lord, the witness, the abode, the refuge, and the friend. I am the origin and the dissolution, the ground, the resting place, and the imperishable seed. I give heat; I withhold and send forth the rain. I am immortality and also death; I am being as well as non-being, O Arjuna.[1]

Moses:

If you follow My laws and faithfully observe My commandments, I will grant your rains in their season, so that the earth shall yield its produce and the trees of the field their fruit. Your threshing shall overtake the vintage, and your vintage shall overtake the sowing; you shall eat your fill of bread and dwell securely in your land.

I will grant peace in the land, and you shall lie down untroubled by anyone; I will give the land respite from vicious beasts, and no sword shall cross your land. . . .

I will look with favor upon you, and make you fertile and multiply you; and I will maintain My covenant with you. . . .

I will establish My abode in your midst, and I will not spurn you. I will be ever present in your midst: I will be your God, and you shall be My people. I the Lord am your God who brought you out from the land of the

Egyptians to be their slaves no more, who broke the bars of your yoke and made you walk erect.[2]

Zoroaster:
When I held You in my mind's eye
then I realised You, O Mazda,
as the First and the Last for all Eternity,
as the Father of the Good Mind,
the true Creator of Truth,
and Lord over the actions of life.[3]

Buddha:
There is, bhikkus,* a not-born, a not-brought-to-being, a not-made, a not-conditioned. If, bhikkhus, there were no not-born, not-brought-to-being, not-made, not-conditioned, no escape would be discerned from what is born, brought-to-being, made, conditioned. But since there is a not-born, a not-brought-to-being, a not-made, a not-conditioned, therefore an escape is discerned from what is born, brought-to-being, made, conditioned.[4]

Jesus Christ:
Therefore I say unto you; Take no thought for your life, what ye shall eat, or what ye shall drink; nor yet for your body, what ye shall put on. Is not the life more than meat, and the body than raiment? Behold the fowls of the air: for they sow not, neither do they reap, nor gather into barns; yet your heavenly Father feedeth them. Are ye not much better than they? Which of you by taking thought can add one cubit unto his stature? And why take you thought for raiment? Consider the lilies of the field, how they grow; they toil not, neither do they spin. And yet I say unto you, That even Solomon in all his glory was not arrayed like one of these. Wherefore if God so clothe the grass of the field, which to day is, and to morrow is cast into the oven, shall he not much more clothe you, O ye of little faith?[5]

* Monks

Muḥammad:

All that is in the Heavens and in the Earth praiseth God, and He is the Mighty, the Wise!

His the Kingdom of the Heavens and of the Earth; He maketh alive and killeth; and He hath power over all things!

He is the first and the last; the Seen and the Hidden; and He knoweth all things!

It is He who in six days created the Heavens and the Earth, then ascended His throne. He knoweth that which entereth the earth, and that which goeth forth from it, and what cometh down from Heaven, and what mounteth up to it; and wherever ye are, He is with you; and God beholdeth all your actions!

His the kingdom of the Heavens and the Earth; and to God shall all things return!

He causeth the night to pass into the day, and He causeth the day to pass into the night: and He knoweth the very secrets of the bosom![6]

Bahá'u'lláh:

To every discerning and illumined heart it is evident that God, the unknowable Essence, the divine Being, is immensely exalted beyond every human attribute, such as corporeal existence, ascent and descent, egress and regress. Far be it from His glory that human tongue should adequately recount His praise, or that human heart comprehend His fathomless mystery. He is and hath ever been veiled in the ancient eternity of His Essence, and will remain in His Reality everlastingly hidden from the sight of men. "No vision taketh in Him, but He taketh in all vision; He is the Subtle, the All Perceiving."* No tie of direct intercourse can possibly bind Him to His creatures. He standeth exalted beyond and above all separation and union, all proximity and remoteness. No sign can indicate His presence or His absence; inasmuch as by a word of His command all that are in heaven and on earth have come to exist, and by His wish, which is the Primal Will itself, all have stepped out of utter nothingness into the realm of being, the world of the visible.[7]

---

* Qur'án 6:103.

And so we find ourselves at the Source of creation. No matter what name or definition is assigned—God, Allah, Mazda, the not-born—it is the Creator that the Manifestations of God call us to obey and worship. God is indeed a fathomless mystery. I urge you to meditate on these passages, and let your heart be lifted by them.

17

Response

In the course of my life, I have passed through increasingly complex phases of development until my present virtuous powers could begin to manifest.

During my time in the womb, physical attributes became apparent, but my limbs and organs were only in an initial phase of growth; their potential could only be realized later, far removed from the protective confines of the womb.

Those little buds of limbs and organs were only hints of future capacity—ears that would someday discern sounds, legs that would someday walk, arms that would someday reach, and hands that would someday grasp. I know this by the wisdom of hindsight, as one who hears, walks, reaches, and grasps. I understand a hand can grasp because I *do* grasp. At the time, however, when my hand was developing, I had no such knowledge. My hand formed; I was oblivious. Nevertheless those fingers pointed to a greater condition than I was presently manifesting, a condition as an independently functioning organism.

The development of my brain, nervous system, and sensory organs showed evidence that an even greater condition was in store for me, a condition that included emotional, cognitive, and intellectual capacities that would allow me to observe, think, and solve complicated problems.

Every phase of development resulted in a new condition and brought me to a higher level of existence. Without that time in the physical phase of development, my development of emotional and cognitive powers would have been impossible. The physical phase prepared me for the emotional and cognitive phase.

No moment of this development was an end in itself. The purpose of each stage of growth was to bring me to an ever greater condition. Each phase was not only the conclusion of the development that had gone before, it was also preparation for the successful continuation of the process.

There is still a part of me undergoing enormous change. Although these capacities are only starting to make their appearance and I stumble about terribly in my attempts to be virtuous, my potential to be virtuous holds the promise of future realization. I don't really understand what my virtues are for. Many people don't bother to develop their virtues at all and see them as superfluous and even as a sign of weakness. The fact is, we won't even know what virtue is actually for until we pass into the life hereafter.

Our developing virtues can be compared to the hand developing in the womb. If I had been conscious in the womb, might I not have looked upon my hand as some strange deformity? Of what use was this thing at the end of my arm with its wriggly little digits? There I was, floating in my liquid universe where everything I needed was provided by a lovely little tube that went right into my belly. In fact, everything I needed *was* the tube and my belly, so if I had the capacity to do so, I might have decided, *I'm going to put all my energies there and let these superfluous little appendages wither.*

And, in a way, I'd have been right. For in the world of the womb those appendages *are* superfluous. But what I couldn't have known, because we don't get to see into the future, is that I would soon need those appendages with their wriggly digits. The fact is, that womb-world is contained by a much larger world. It's just that in the prenatal stage of development, I was totally unaware of its existence. I had no way of knowing that life without hands in the next phase of my existence would make things very difficult for me. The requirements of the world that contains my womb-world are quite different from the requirements of the womb-world.

My stay in the womb-world was a short one, and I only spent enough time there to safely complete the initial phase of my development. My stay in this world is a short one, too, and I only spend time in it to continue that development.

My virtuous powers can be compared to the fetus's hand—small, delicate, partially formed, incomplete, immature. I only have a very vague idea as to what my virtuous power is for. I do know that when I work with it, exercise it, and do what I can to aid its development, new dimensions open up within me—dimensions I can only describe as feeling connected to something greater than myself. This "something greater" is wonderfully warm and attractive and feels, in the depths of my heart, like pure love.

This is just the beginning, I know. I may not understand what virtue is for, but that's only because I can't see into the future. It's only because I am ignorant about the greater world that contains this world. I have no way of knowing how difficult my existence will be in that world if I spend all my energies on those things pertinent only to this material world and allow my virtuous powers to wither.

The Manifestations of God have clearly warned us of the consequences of neglecting the virtuous part of our development. They also speak of a joyous future if we *do* attend to virtuous development.

We are conscious creatures, and our minds and hearts are diverted by many things. We have the power of free will, and each individual must choose for himself or herself how to respond to what the Manifestations of God have placed before us. Divine Revelation acts as both sun and rain to the germinating capacities of the soul, infusing us with a love that is divine.

But this love can only reach us when we turn our hearts to it. In fact, while the earliest phases of development did not require free will, this phase does, and it is imperative that we willingly take that first step.

Bahá'u'lláh tells us: *"Love Me, that I may love thee. If thou lovest Me not, My love can in no wise reach thee."*[1] And so we find we are faced with a choice. Do we turn toward what the Manifestations of God offer, or do we turn away? Do we accept? Or do we reject?

Acceptance is not the easiest of paths. It is a path of continual development; therefore, it is a path of continual effort. The steps are wobbly ones, to say the least. But think about how development unfolds. Consider how hard you've had to work from the time of conception, what tender sprouts your powers were at the outset of each phase of development. Remember that you had to *use* these powers and *exercise* them, to help them develop.

In light of all this, shouldn't you expect to work at this phase, too, and be terribly bad at it? Shouldn't you expect that you might miss the mark from time to time, fall on your virtuous bottom, but get back up and keep going? At least you can be assured that acting with virtue is the ultimate act of consciousness, the crowning human achievement, and the tip of the developmental arrow that launches you into the next phase of existence.

And here is the wonderful part. We are not alone in this process. The Manifestations of God point out the way, inspire us, comfort us, and keep us focused on the goal. They have appeared repeatedly to reinvigorate the personal process and help guide us collectively into the next phase of human evolution.

At this time in history, Bahá'u'lláh has taught that the time is at hand to usher in the next phase of humanity's development, during which the oneness of humanity will become fully recognized.

Here and now you stand at the horizon with one foot in the material world and one foot in the spiritual world. Behind you is what you were. Ahead of you is what you have the potential to become. Here and now you make the choice. Do you accept? Or do you reject? In which direction will your next step take you?

Appendix 1

The Soul and Life after Death

Excerpts from *Gleanings from the Writings of Bahá'u'lláh*

It is clear and evident that when the veils that conceal the realities of the manifestations of the Names and Attributes of God, nay of all created things visible or invisible, have been rent asunder, nothing except the Sign of God will remain—a sign which He, Himself, hath placed within these realities. This sign will endure as long as is the wish of the Lord thy God, the Lord of the heavens and of the earth. If such be the blessings conferred on all created things, how superior must be the destiny of the true believer, whose existence and life are to be regarded as the originating purpose of all creation. Just as the conception of faith hath existed from the beginning that hath no beginning, and will endure till the end that hath no end, in like manner will the true believer eternally live and endure. His spirit will everlastingly circle round the Will of God. He will last as long as God, Himself, will last. He is revealed through the Revelation of God, and is hidden at His bidding. It is evident that the loftiest mansions in the Realm of Immortality have been ordained as the habitation of them that have truly believed in God and in His signs. Death can never invade that holy seat. Thus have We entrusted thee with the signs of Thy Lord, that thou mayest persevere in thy love for Him, and be of them that comprehend this truth. (section 73)

Thou hast asked Me whether man, as apart from the Prophets of God and His chosen ones, will retain, after his physical death, the self-same individuality, personality, consciousness, and understanding that characterize his life in this world. If this should be the case, how is it, thou hast observed, that whereas such slight injuries to his mental faculties as fainting and severe illness deprive him of his understanding and consciousness, his death, which must involve the decomposition of his body and the dissolution of its elements, is powerless to destroy that understanding and extinguish that consciousness? How can any one imagine that man's consciousness and personality will be maintained, when the very instruments necessary to their existence and function will have completely disintegrated?

Know thou that the soul of man is exalted above, and is independent of all infirmities of body or mind. That a sick person showeth signs of weakness is due to the hindrances that interpose themselves between his soul and his body, for the soul itself remaineth unaffected by any bodily ailments. Consider the light of the lamp. Though an external object may interfere with its radiance, the light itself continueth to shine with undiminished power. In like manner, every malady afflicting the body of man is an impediment that preventeth the soul from manifesting its inherent might and power. When it leaveth the body, however, it will evince such ascendancy, and reveal such influence as no force on earth can equal. Every pure, every refined and sanctified soul will be endowed with tremendous power, and shall rejoice with exceeding gladness.

Consider the lamp which is hidden under a bushel. Though its light be shining, yet its radiance is concealed from men. Likewise, consider the sun which hath been obscured by the clouds. Observe how its splendor appeareth to have diminished, when in reality the source of that light hath remained unchanged. The soul of man should be likened unto this sun, and all things on earth should be regarded as his body. So long as no external impediment interveneth between them, the body will, in its entirety, continue to reflect the light of the soul, and to be sustained by its power. As soon as, however, a veil interposeth itself between them, the brightness of that light seemeth to lessen.

Consider again the sun when it is completely hidden behind the clouds. Though the earth is still illumined with its light, yet the measure of light which it receiveth is considerably reduced. Not until the clouds have dispersed, can the sun shine again in the plenitude of its glory. Neither the presence of the cloud nor its absence can, in any way, affect the inherent splendor of the sun. The soul of man is the sun by which his body is illumined, and from which it draweth its sustenance, and should be so regarded.

Consider, moreover, how the fruit, ere it is formed, lieth potentially within the tree. Were the tree to be cut into pieces, no sign nor any part of the fruit, however small, could be detected. When it appeareth, however, it manifesteth itself, as thou hast observed, in its wondrous beauty and glorious perfection. Certain fruits, indeed, attain their fullest development only after being severed from the tree. (section 80)

And now concerning thy question regarding the soul of man and its survival after death. Know thou of a truth that the soul, after its separation from the body, will continue to progress until it attaineth the presence of God, in a state and condition which neither the revolution of ages and centuries, nor the changes and chances of this world, can alter. It will endure as long as the Kingdom of God, His sovereignty, His dominion and power will endure. It will manifest the signs of God and His attributes, and will reveal His loving kindness and bounty. The movement of My Pen is stilled when it attempteth to befittingly describe the loftiness and glory of so exalted a station. The honor with which the Hand of Mercy will invest the soul is such as no tongue can adequately reveal, nor any other earthly agency describe. Blessed is the soul which, at the hour of its separation from the body, is sanctified from the vain imaginings of the peoples of the world. Such a soul liveth and moveth in accordance with the Will of its Creator, and entereth the all-highest Paradise. The Maids of Heaven, inmates of the loftiest mansions, will circle around it, and the Prophets of God and His chosen ones will seek its companionship. With them that soul will freely converse, and will recount unto them that which it hath been made to endure in the path of God, the Lord of all worlds. If any man be told that which hath been ordained for such a soul in the worlds of God, the Lord of the throne on high and of earth below, his whole being will instantly blaze out in his great longing to attain that most exalted, that sanctified and resplendent station. . . . The nature of the soul after death can never be described, nor is it meet and permissible to reveal its whole character to the eyes of men. The Prophets and Messengers of God have been sent down for the sole purpose of guiding mankind to the straight Path of Truth. The purpose underlying their revelation hath been to educate all men, that they may, at the hour of death, ascend, in the utmost purity and sanctity and with absolute detachment, to the throne of the Most High. The light which these souls radiate is responsible for the progress of the world and the advancement of its peoples. They are like unto leaven which leaveneth the world of being, and constitute the animating force through which the arts and wonders of the world are made manifest. Through them the clouds rain their bounty upon men, and the earth bringeth forth its fruits. All things must needs have a cause, a motive power, an animating principle. These souls and symbols of detachment have provided, and will continue to provide, the supreme moving impulse in the world of being. The world beyond is as different from this world as this world is different from that of the child while still in the womb of its mother. When the soul attaineth the Presence of God, it will assume the form that best befitteth its immortality and is worthy of its celestial habitation. Such an existence is a contingent and not an absolute existence, inasmuch as the former is preceded by a cause, whilst the latter is independent thereof. Absolute existence is strictly confined to God, exalted be His glory. Well is it with them that apprehend this truth. Wert thou to ponder in thine heart the behavior of the Prophets of God thou wouldst assuredly and readily testify that there must needs be other worlds besides this world. The majority of the truly wise and learned have, throughout the ages, as it hath been recorded by the Pen of Glory in the Tablet of Wisdom, borne witness to the truth of that which the holy Writ of God hath revealed. Even the materialists have testified in their writings to the wisdom of these divinely-appointed Messengers, and have regarded the references made by the Prophets to Paradise, to hell fire, to future reward and punishment, to have been actuated by a desire to educate and uplift the souls of men. Consider, therefore, how the generality of mankind, whatever their beliefs or theories, have recognized the excellence, and admitted the superiority of these Prophets of God. These Gems of Detachment are acclaimed by some as the embodiments of wisdom, while others believe them to be the mouthpiece of God Himself. How could such Souls have consented to surrender themselves unto their enemies if they believed all the worlds of God to have been reduced to this earthly life? Would they have willingly suffered such afflictions and torments as no man hath ever experienced or witnessed? (section 81)

Thou hast asked Me concerning the nature of the soul. Know, verily, that the soul is a sign of God, a heavenly gem whose reality the most learned of men hath failed to grasp, and whose mystery no mind, however acute, can ever hope to unravel. It is the first among all created things to declare the excellence of its Creator, the first to recognize His glory, to cleave to His truth, and to bow down in adoration before Him. If it be faithful to God, it will reflect His light, and will, eventually, return unto Him. If it fail, however, in its allegiance to its Creator, it will become a victim to self and passion, and will, in the end, sink in their depths.

Whoso hath, in this Day, refused to allow the doubts and fancies of men to turn him away from Him Who is the Eternal Truth, and hath not suffered the tumult provoked by the ecclesiastical and secular authorities to deter him from recognizing His Message, such a man will be regarded by God, the Lord of all men, as one of His mighty signs, and will be numbered among them whose names have been inscribed by the Pen of the Most High in His Book. Blessed is he that hath recognized the true stature of such a soul, that hath acknowledged its station, and discovered its virtues.

. . . Verily I say, the human soul is, in its essence, one of the signs of God, a mystery among His mysteries. It is one of the mighty signs of the Almighty, the harbinger that proclaimeth the reality of all the worlds of God. Within it lieth concealed that which the world is now utterly incapable of apprehending. Ponder in thine heart the revelation of the Soul of God that pervadeth all His Laws, and contrast it with that base and appetitive nature that hath rebelled against Him, that forbiddeth men to turn unto the Lord of Names, and impelleth them to walk after their lusts and wickedness. Such a soul hath, in truth, wandered far in the path of error. (section 82)

Appendix 2

Some Virtues and Their Definitions

Acceptance	favorable reception; to receive as adequate or satisfactory
Assertiveness	the quality or state of being disposed to, or characterized by, bold or confident expression
Balance	emotional equilibrium; to achieve a state or position between extremes
Caring	having regard for the needs or feelings of others
Chastity	morally pure; decent; modest
Cleanliness	the quality or state of being habitually and carefully neat and clean
Compassion	the deep feeling of sharing the suffering of another in the inclination to give aid or support, to show mercy
Confidence	a feeling of assurance or certainty, especially concerning oneself
Consideration	the quality of showing thoughtful and sympathetic regard for others
Contentment	the quality or state of not desiring more than what one has; satisfaction; resignation to circumstances
Courage	the quality of mind and spirit that enables one to face danger with self-possession; confidence, and resolution; bravery; valor
Courtesy	polite behavior; gracious manners
Creativity	the quality of being able to create or bring into being
Detachment	freedom from prejudice or bias; aloofness or indifference to worldly concerns

Determination	the quality or state of being resolute or marked by firmness of purpose
Devotion	the state of being ardently dedicated or attached to a person or cause; faithfulness, loyalty; religious ardor or zeal; piety
Diligence	attentive care; persistent effort
Discernment	the quality or state of being keenly or discriminatingly astute, perceptive
Efficiency	the quality of acting or producing effectively with a minimum of waste, expense or unnecessary effort
Enthusiasm	eagerness, zeal
Excellence	the quality of being better than or surpassing; outdoing (going beyond a limit or standard)
Faithfulness	the state of being dutiful and loyal; worthy of trust or credence; consistently reliable; consistent with truth or actuality; accurate, exact
Flexibility	characterized by responsiveness to change; adaptable
Forgiveness	the act of excusing for a fault or offense; the act of renouncing anger or resentment against an offender
Friendliness	the quality of being favorably disposed, not antagonistic; warm, comforting
Gentleness	the quality or state of being considerate; amiable; patient; mild
Grace	a disposition to be generous or helpful; goodwill
Helpfulness	service, assistance, or aid
Honesty	fairness, honor, integrity; not lying, cheating, stealing, or taking unfair advantage; honorable, truthful, trustworthy; genuine
Humility	the quality or state of being modest, unpretentious
Idealism	pursuit of one's ideals
Integrity	probity; the state of being unimpaired; soundness; completeness
Joyfulness	high pleasure or delight; happiness, gladness
Justice	moral rightness, equity, honor, fairness
Kindness	the quality of being friendly, generous or hospitable, warm-hearted, good

Love	faithfulness, the benevolence, kindness, or brotherhood that one should rightfully feel toward others
Loyalty	faithful to a person, ideal, or custom; feelings of devoted attachment and affection
Mercy	kind and compassionate treatment of an offender, enemy, prisoner, or other person under one's power; clemency
Moderation	not excessive or extreme; opposed to radical or extreme views or measures
Modesty	freedom from pretentiousness; moderate, not extreme
Obedience	the quality or state of being obedient (i.e., to carry out or fulfill a command, order, or instruction of; to carry out or comply with)
Openness	willing to hear and consider; free from reserve or pretense
Orderliness	tidiness; the quality or state of being without violence or disruption; peacefulness; methodicalness
Patience	the capacity, habit, or state of calm endurance
Peacefulness	the quality or state of being undisturbed by strife, turmoil, or disagreement; tranquillity
Perseverance	the capacity or condition of holding to a course of action, belief, or purpose without giving way
Piety	devotion or reverence to God
Prayerfulness	the quality or state of devotion or communion with God
Purity	freedom from sin or guilt, innocence; chastity
Purposefulness	the quality or state of having or manifesting a purpose (object toward which one strives or for which something exists; goal, aim)
Reliability	the quality or state of being dependable
Respect	to feel or show esteem for; to honor; to show consideration for; to avoid violation of; to treat with deference
Responsibility	the quality or state of being capable of making moral or rational decisions on one's own and, therefore, answerable for one's behavior
Reverence	a feeling of profound awe and respect and often of love; veneration

Righteousness	the quality or state of meeting the standard of what is right and just
Sacrifice	the forfeiture of something highly valued, such as an idea, object, or friendship, for the sake of someone or something considered to have a greater value or claim
Self-Discipline	regulation or correction of one's own behavior
Service	work done for others as an occupation or business; an act of assistance or benefit to another or others; favor
Simplicity	the state of being simple, without artifice, unembellished; free of pretense or guile
Steadfastness	the state of being firmly loyal or constant, unswerving
Tact	the ability to appreciate the delicacy of a situation and to do or say the kindest or most fitting thing; diplomacy
Tenderness	the act of treating with tender regard
Thankfulness	the quality or state of being grateful
Tolerance	the capacity for or practice of allowing or respecting the nature, beliefs, or behaviors of others
Trustworthiness	the quality or state of warranting trust; being dependable, reliable
Understanding	the power of perceiving and comprehending
Willingness	inclined or favorably disposed to accept or tolerate; consenting; acquiescent
Wisdom	understanding of what is true, right, or lasting; good sense
Wonder	to have a feeling of awe or admiration

Notes

Introduction
1. Imam Alí, quoted in Bahá'u'lláh, *The Seven Valleys and the Four Valleys*, 34.

2 / Dividing the Universal Pie
1. Margulis, Lynn, and Karlene V. Schwartz, *Five Kingdoms: An Illustrated Guide to the Phyla of Life on Earth*, p. 4.

3 / A New Model
1. 'Abdu'l-Bahá, *The Promulgation of Universal Peace*, pp. 336–37.

2. Please see *Encyclopaedia Britannica Online*, www.britannica.com/EBchecked/topic/574576/string-theory.

3. Ritchie, David, *The Encyclopedia of Earthquakes and Volcanoes*, Facts on File, New York, p. 166.

6 / Human Development: The Emotional and Cognitive Stage
1. Leach, Penelope, *Your Baby and Child, From Birth to Age Five*, p. 138.

8 / Human Development: The Virtuous Stage
1. Luke 10:30–35.
2. Luke 10:25–29.
3. Luke 10:36.
4. Luke 10:37.
5. Ibid.

10 / Search

1. Bahá'u'lláh, *Gleanings*, no. 122.
2. Ibid, no. 27.4–5.
3. Ibid, no. 21.

11 / Virtuous Educators

1. The New Encyclopaedia Britannica, "Krishna," Volume 7, p. 7; Sri Swami Satchidananda, *The Living Gita: The Complete Bhagavad Gita.*
2. Exodus 3:5–10.
3. Matthew 3:16–17.
4. Sura 96:1–5.
5. Bahá'u'lláh, *Epistle to the Son of the Wolf,* p. 21.
6. Bahá'u'lláh, The Hidden Words, Arabic no. 1.

12 / . . . And Do Good

1. Bahá'u'lláh, *Gleanings*, no. 27.4, 27.5.
2. Ibid., no. 27.4.
3. *Bhagavadgita*, p. 69.
4. Leviticus 19.
5. Gathas, Yasna 33:2–5.
6. *Buddhist Scriptures*, pp. 185–86.
7. Luke 6:27–38.
8. Sura 4:40–44.
9. Bahá'u'lláh, *Gleanings*, no. 130.

13 / Reward and Punishment

1. *Bhagavadgita*, pp. 74–75.
2. Deuteronomy 30:15–20.
3. Gathas, Yasna 31:20–21.
4. Dhammapada, v. 15–18.
5. Matthew 25:31–46.
6. Sura 92.
7. Bahá'u'lláh, *Gleanings,* no. 86.

14 / Divine Revelation

1. Bahá'u'lláh, *Gleanings*, no. 122.1.
2. Ibid, no. 34.1.
3. Ibid, no. 34.2.

4. Ibid, no. 90.2.

5. Ibid, no. 34.3.

6. Bhagavadgita 4:9.

7. Exodus 3:7–14.

8. Yasna 29:8.

9. *Ariyapariyesana Sutta, The Noble Search: The Middle Length Discourses of the Buddha*, p. 263.

10. Matthew 11:27–29.

11. Sura 53:1–12.

12. Bahá'u'lláh, *Summons of the Lord of Hosts*, "Súriy-i-Haykal," ¶182.

13. Matthew 7:16.

14. *Bhagavadgita*, p. 35.

15. Exodus 4:10–12.

16. Yasna 43:11–12.

17. *Buddhist Scriptures*, pp. 165–66.

18. John 12:49.

19. Sura 10:16.

20. Bahá'u'lláh, quoted in Shoghi Effendi, *God Passes By*, p. 102.

15 / Oneness

1. *Bhagavadgita*, p. 21; Isaiah 9:6; *All Things Made New*, Dinkird, a late collection of traditional Zoroastrian scripture; *Buddhist Scriptures*, pp. 20, 237; John 16:12–13; *Muhammad and the Course of Islam*, p. 244; *Gleanings,* no. 145; *Tablets of Bahá'u'lláh*, p. 161.

2. Bahá'u'lláh, *Gleanings*, nos. 31.1, 27.5.

16 / God

1. Bhagavadgita 9:4–19.

2. Leviticus 26:3–13.

3. Yasna 31:8.

4. Ireland, *The Udana & The Itivuttaka: Two Classics from the Pali Canon*, p. 103.

5. Matthew 6:25–30.

6. Sura 57:1–6.

7. Bahá'u'lláh, The Kitáb-i-Íqán, ¶104.

17 / Response

1. Bahá'u'lláh, The Hidden Words, Arabic no. 5.

Bibliography

Works by Bahá'u'lláh

Epistle to the Son of the Wolf. Translated by Shoghi Effendi. 1st pocket-sized ed. Wilmette, IL: Bahá'í Publishing Trust, 1988.

Gleanings from the Writings of Bahá'u'lláh. New ed. Translated by Shoghi Effendi. Wilmette, IL: Bahá'í Publishing, 2005.

The Hidden Words. Translated by Shoghi Effendi. Wilmette, IL: Bahá'í Publishing, 2002.

The Kitáb-i-Aqdas: The Most Holy Book. Wilmette, IL: Bahá'í Publishing Trust, 1992.

The Kitáb-i-Íqán: The Book of Certitude. Translated by Shoghi Effendi. Wilmette, IL: Bahá'í Publishing, 2003.

Prayers and Meditations. Translated from the original Persian and Arabic by Shoghi Effendi. 1st pocket-size ed. Wilmette, IL: Bahá'í Publishing Trust, 1987.

The Summons of the Lord of Hosts: Tablets of Bahá'u'lláh. Wilmette, IL: Bahá'í Publishing, 2006.

Tablets of Bahá'u'lláh revealed after the Kitáb-i-Aqdas. Compiled by the Research Department of the Universal House of Justice. Translated by Habib Taherzadeh et al. Wilmette, IL: Bahá'í Publishing Trust, 1988.

Works by 'Abdu'l-Bahá

The Promulgation of Universal Peace: Talks Delivered by 'Abdu'l-Bahá During His Visit to the United States and Canada in 1912. Compiled by Howard MacNutt. New ed. Wilmette, IL: Bahá'í Publishing Trust, 2007.

Selections from the Writings of 'Abdu'l-Bahá. Compiled by the Research Department of the Universal House of Justice. Translated by a Committee at the Bahá'í World Center and Marzieh Gail. Wilmette, IL: Bahá'í Publishing Trust, 1997.

Works by Shoghi Effendi
God Passes By. New edition. Wilmette, IL: Bahá'í Publishing Trust, 1974.

Bahá'í Compilations
Bahá'í Prayers: A Selection of Prayers Revealed by Bahá'u'lláh, the Báb, and 'Abdu'l-Bahá. Wilmette, IL: Bahá'í Publishing Trust, 2002.

Other Works
Abú'l-Faḍl, Mírzá. *Miracles & Metaphors*. Translated by Juan Ricardo Cole. Los Angeles: Kalimát Press, 1981.

———. *The Brilliant Proof*. Originally published as "The Brilliant Proof," in Chicago by the Bahá'í News Service, 1912. Los Angeles: Kalimát Press, 1998.

The American Heritage Dictionary of the English Language. New York: American Heritage Publishing and Houghton Mifflin, 1973.

Armstrong, Karen. *Buddha*. New York: Viking Press, 2001.

Balyuzi, H. M. *Muhammad and the Course of Islam*, Oxford: George Ronald, 1976.

———. *Bahá'u'lláh: The King of Glory*. Revised ed. Oxford: George Ronald, 1991.

Barry, Robert. *A Theory of Almost Everything: A Scientific and Religious Quest for Ultimate Answers*. Oxford: Oneworld, 1993.

Behe, Michael J. *Darwin's Black Box: The Biochemical Challenge to Evolution*. New York: The Free Press, 1996.

Bhagavadgita. Translated by Sir Edwin Arnold. 1885. Reprint, New York: Dover Publications, 1993.

Blomfield, Lady. *The Chosen Highway*. Wilmette, IL: Bahá'í Publishing Trust, 1975.

Boorstin, D. J. *The Discoverers: A History of Man's Search to Know His World and Himself.* New York: Random House, 1983.

Brazelton, M.D., T. Berry, and Stanley I. Greenspan, M.D. *The Irreducible Needs of Children: What Every Child Must Have to Grow, Learn, and Flourish*. Cambridge, MA: Perseus Publishing, 2000.

Coles, Robert. *The Moral Intelligence of Children*. New York: Random House, 1997.

Compton's Pictured Encyclopedia and Fact-Index. Vol. 2, *Buddha*. Chicago: F. E. Compton Co., Division of Encyclopaedia Britannica, Inc., 1965.

———. Vol. 9, *Moses*. Chicago: F. E. Compton Co., Division of Encyclopaedia Britannica, Inc., 2002.

———. Vol. 15, *Zoroaster*. Chicago: F. E. Compton Co., Division of Encyclopaedia Britannica, Inc., 2002.

Conze, Edward, trans. "The Diamond Sutra." Chap. 3 in *Buddhist Scriptures*. Penguin Books, 1959.

Cunningham, Bill, M.S. *Child Development*. New York: HarperCollins, 1993.

Davis, Kenneth C. *Don't Know Much About the Bible: Everything You Need to Know About the Good Book but Never Learned*. New York: Avon Books, 1999.

Einstein, Albert. *Relativity: The Special and the General Theory*. New York: Crown Trade Paperbacks, 1961.

Ferraby, John. *All Things Made New: A Comprehensive Outline of the Bahá'í Faith*. Wilmette, IL: Bahá'í Publishing Trust, 1963.

Foster, Robert J. *General Geology*. Columbus, OH: Charles E. Merrill Publishing Company, 1969.

Fozdar, Jamshed. *The God of Buddha*. Arricia, Italy: Casa Editrice Bahá'í, 1995.

Frankl, Viktor E. *Man's Search for Meaning*. Revised and Updated. New York: Washington Square Press, 1984.

Gail, Marzieh. *Six Lessons on Islam*. Wilmette, IL: Bahá'í Publishing Trust, 1957.

Gopnick, Alison, PhD, Andrew N. Meltzoff, PhD, and Patricia K. Kuhl, PhD *The Scientist in the Crib: Minds, Brains, and How Children Learn*. New York: William Morrow and Company, 1999.

Hatcher, John S. *The Divine Art of Revelation*. Wilmette, IL: Bahá'í Publishing Trust, 1998.

———. *The Purpose of Physical Reality*. Wilmette, IL: Bahá'í Publishing Trust, 1987.

Hatcher, John S., and William Hatcher. *The Law of Love Enshrined*. Oxford: George Ronald, 1996.

Hatcher, William S. *Love, Power, and Justice: The Dynamics of Authentic Morality*. Wilmette, IL: Bahá'í Publishing Trust, 1998.

———. *The Science of Religion*. 2nd ed. Ottawa, ON: Canadian Association for the Studies on the Bahá'í Faith, 1980.

Hawkes, Jacquetta, and Sir Leonard Woolley. *History of Mankind: Cultural and Scientific Development*. Vol. 1, *Prehistory and the Beginning of Civilization*. New York: Harper & Row, 1963.

The Holy Bible. Authorized King James Version. World Bible Publishers.

Ireland, John D., trans. *The Udana & The Itivuttaka: Two Classics from the Pali Canon.* Kandy, Sri Lanka: Buddhist Publication Society, 1997

Kagan, Jerome. *The Nature of the Child.* New York: Basic Books, 1984.

Khur, Anjam. *The Universe Within: An Exploration of the Human Spirit.* Oxford: Oneworld, 1995.

The Koran. 1909. Translated by J. M. Rodwell. Reprint, London: Everyman, 1994.

Lickona, Thomas. *Raising Good Children: Helping Your Child Through the Stages of Moral Development.* New York: Bantam Books, 1983.

Margulis, Lynn, and Karlene V. Schwartz. *Five Kingdoms: An Illustrated Guide to the Phyla of Life on Earth.* New York: W. H. Freeman and Company, 1988.

Murchie, Guy. *The Seven Mysteries of Life: An Exploration of Science and Philosophy.* Boston: Houghton Mifflin, 1978.

Ñanamoli, Bhikku and Bhikkhu Bodhi, trans. *The Middle Length Discourses of the Buddha.* A New Translation of the Majjhima Nikaya. Somerville, MA: Wisdom Publications, 1995.

Nanavutty, Piloo, trans. *The Gathas of Zarathushtra: Hymns in Praise of Wisdom.* Middleton, NJ: Grantha Corporation, 1999.

O'Brien, Maureen, and Sherill Tippins. *Watch Me Grow, I'm Two: Every Parent's Guide to the Lively and Challenging 24- to 36-month-old.* New York: HarperCollins, 2001.

Pinker, Steven. *The Language Instinct: How the Mind Creates Language.* New York: William Morrow and Company, 1994.

Porter, J. R. *Jesus Christ: The Jesus of History, the Christ of Faith.* New York: Oxford University Press, 1999.

Radhakrishnan, Sarvepalli, and Charles Moore, eds. "Bhagavad-gita, The." Chap. 3 in *A Sourcebook in Indian Philosophy.* Princeton, NJ: Princeton University Press, 1957.

———. "Dhammapada, The." Chap. 9 in *A Sourcebook in Indian Philosophy.* Princeton, NJ: Princeton University Press, 1957.

Reuban, Steven Carr. *Raising Ethical Children: 10 Keys to Helping Your Children Become Moral and Caring.* Rocklin, CA: Prima Publishing, 1994.

Ridley, Matt. *Nature Via Nurture.* New York: HarperCollins, 2003.

Ruhe, David S. *Robe of Light: The Persian Years of the Supreme Prophet Bahá'u'lláh, 1817–1853.* Oxford: George Ronald, 1994.

Ryan, Kevin, and Karen E. Bohlin. *Building Character in Schools: Practical Ways to Bring Moral Instruction to Life.* San Francisco: Jossey-Bass, 1999.

Rymer, Russ. *Genie: An Abused Child's Flight from Silence.* New York: HarperCollins, 1994.

Salvi, Julio. *The Eternal Quest for God.* Oxford: George Ronald, 1989.

Sours, Michael. *The Station and Claims of Bahá'u'lláh.* Wilmette, IL: Bahá'í Publishing Trust, 1997.

Taherzadeh, Adib. *The Revelation of Bahá'u'lláh.* Vol. 1, *Baghdad, 1853–63.* Oxford: George Ronald, 1974.

———. *The Revelation of Bahá'u'lláh.* Vol. 2, *Adrianople, 1863–68.* Oxford: George Ronald, 1977.

The Torah: The Five Books of Moses. Philadelphia: Jewish Publication Society of America, 1962.

Van Tyll, Hendrick. *The Parables: The Forgotten Message.* Pelham, AL: Middle Street Communications, 1993.

Verny, Thomas, M.D., and John Kelly. *The Secret Life of the Unborn Child.* New York: Summit Books, 1981.

Villee, Claude A. *Biology.* Philadelphia: W. B. Saunders Company, 1972.

Walker, Alan, and Pat Shipman. *The Wisdom of the Bones: In Search of Human Origins.* New York: Alfred A. Knopf, 1996.

Wenke, Robert J. *Patterns in Prehistory: Humankind's First Three Million Years.* 2nd ed. Oxford: Oxford University Press, 1984.

Wilson, James Q. *The Moral Sense.* New York: The Free Press, 1993.

Index

Bahá'í Publishing and the Bahá'í Faith

Bahá'í Publishing produces books based on the teachings of the Bahá'í Faith. Founded over 160 years ago, the Bahá'í Faith has spread to some 235 nations and territories and is now accepted by more than five million people. The word "Bahá'í" means "follower of Bahá'u'lláh." Bahá'u'lláh, the founder of the Bahá'í Faith, asserted that He is the Messenger of God for all of humanity in this day. The cornerstone of His teachings is the establishment of the spiritual unity of humankind, which will be achieved by personal transformation and the application of clearly identified spiritual principles. Bahá'ís also believe that there is but one religion and that all the Messengers of God—among them Abraham, Zoroaster, Moses, Krishna, Buddha, Jesus, and Muḥammad—have progressively revealed its nature. Together, the world's great religions are expressions of a single, unfolding divine plan. Human beings, not God's Messengers, are the source of religious divisions, prejudices, and hatreds.

The Bahá'í Faith is not a sect or denomination of another religion, nor is it a cult or a social movement. Rather, it is a globally recognized independent world religion founded on new books of scripture revealed by Bahá'u'lláh.

Bahá'í Publishing is an imprint of the National Spiritual Assembly of the Bahá'ís of the United States.

For more information about the Bahá'í Faith,
or to contact Bahá'ís near you, visit
http://www.bahai.us/
or call
1-800-22-unite

Other Books Available from Bahá'í Publishing

Creative Dimensions of Suffering
A-M. Ghadirian, M.D.
$15.00 U.S. / $17.00 CAN
Trade Paper
ISBN 978-1-931847-60-5

A noted professor and psychiatrist explores the link between suffering, creativity, and spirituality

Creative Dimensions of Suffering draws upon the author's personal knowledge and experience as a psychiatrist, as well as extensive research in literature, to explore the enigmatic and intriguing connection between creativity and suffering. He examines the lives of many artists, writers, poets, and scientists, as well as ordinary individuals, who have risen above their own suffering and left behind a legacy of unique and amazing experiences. Among these are well-known figures such as van Gogh, Tchaikovsky, Beethoven, Helen Keller, and Christopher Reeve. Examining their lives for insight into how they dealt with their adversity through creativity, he also explores how various conditions such as alcoholism, depression, bipolar disorder, and dementia can influence a person's creative impulse and how the interplay of creativity and spirituality can help a person deal with trauma and hardship.

Drawing on principles found in the teachings of the Bahá'í Faith, Dr. Ghadirian considers the meaning of suffering, its place in human society, and how it can lead to a closer, happier relationship with God, as well as a better relationship with oneself and with others. Indeed, many of those who have suffered the most in life have found new meaning through adversity and have emerged victorious. Their encounters with adversity and their victory over it suggest the presence of another force beyond understanding that reinforces the individual during periods of intense suffering.

High Desert
A Journey of Survival and Hope
Kim Douglas
$20.00 U.S. / $22.00 CAN
Trade Paper
ISBN 978-1-931847-59-9

A deeply moving memoir with a holistic approach to overcoming the effects of growing up in a severely abusive home

High Desert is a courageous, gripping, and deeply personal autobiographical account about growing up in an abusive home and finding a path to recovery by learning to rely on faith and spiritual beliefs to heal and grow in ways that go beyond traditional twelve-step programs and other approaches. In this eye-opening account, Kim Douglas reveals a wide range of issues and behaviors that will be familiar to many who have come from similar circumstances: eating disorders, obsessive or compulsive behaviors, and troubled relationships with friends and family members. Most important is the author's insight and experience in finding effective ways of coping with life's challenges, learning to trust others in a close relationship, parenting without repeating the cycle of abuse, healing the relationship with the abuser, and forgiving those who don't help in a time of crisis.

Illumine My Family
Prayers and Meditations from the Bahá'í Faith
Bahá'u'lláh, the Báb, and 'Abdu'l-Bahá
Compiled by Bahá'í Publishing
$12.00 U.S. / $13.50 CAN
Trade Paper
ISBN 978-1-931847-62-9

A heartwarming collection of prayers for people of all faiths to meet the challenges of everyday life

Illumine My Family is a collection of prayers and meditative passages from the writings of the Bahá'í Faith that will help any family wishing to incorporate spirituality into their daily lives. The passages included offer guidance and prayers on subjects relevant to any family regardless of their background or current circumstances. Subjects covered include marriage, parents, motherhood, children, love, healing, the loss of a loved one, and more. The book has been put together with the hope that it will assist families to grow together and to foster strong relationships with each other and with God.

Life at First Sight
Finding the Divine in the Details
Phyllis Edgerly Ring
$15.00 U.S. / $17.00 CAN
Trade Paper
ISBN 978-1-931847-67-4

Phyllis Ring divulges in this collection of personal essays how to "see the spiritual" in everyday moments and everyday life. Like love at first sight, "life at first sight" focuses on instant recognition and irresistible attraction, a sense of something mysteriously familiar and a sense of spiritual connection. The essays show how to develop a new sense of being during daily activities and everyday interactions, as well as through engagement with the natural world. As a jumping-off point for spiritual conversation, these compositions offer food for thought on how to lead a more spiritual life.

". . . Captures the web of meaning that unites and sustains all of human life. These sparkling essays remind us that the spiritual side of life is not a luxury or an optional nicety, but utterly crucial. At this moment in history, no message is more vital."—Larry Dossey, MD, Author of *The Power of Premonitions* and *The Extraordinary Healing Power of Ordinary Things*

"These essays are a treasure, especially as they pursue the journey of the human spirit through the perils—and joys—of 'the road not taken.' This is the sort of book that will warm, celebrate, and console the reader on a sour day. The book is lovingly written and beautifully conceived, and dares to approach the practical reality of the spiritual life."—Dolores Kendrick, Poet Laureate of the District of Columbia and Author of *Why the Woman Is Singing on the Corner* and *Now Is the Thing to Praise*

To view our complete catalog,
Please visit http://books.bahai.us